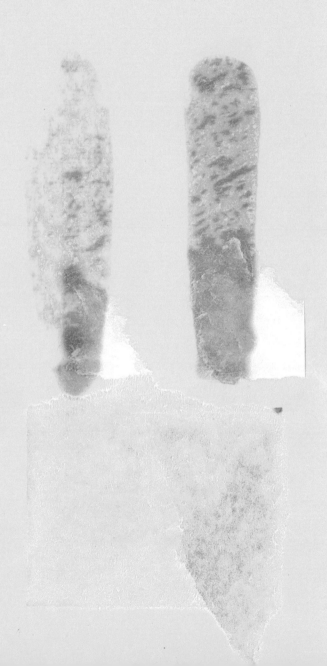

A HISTORY OF PHILOSOPHY
Volume 1
ANTIQUITY AND THE MIDDLE AGES

A HISTORY
OF
PHILOSOPHY

Volume 1

Antiquity and the Middle Ages

ANDERS WEDBERG

CLARENDON PRESS · OXFORD

1982

Oxford University Press, Walton Street, Oxford OX2 6DP

London Glasgow New York Toronto
Delhi Bombay Calcutta Madras Karachi
Kuala Lumpur Singapore Hong Kong Tokyo
Nairobi Dar es Salaam Cape Town
Melbourne Auckland

and associate companies in
Beirut Berlin Ibadan Mexico City

Published in the United States by
Oxford University Press, New York

First published 1958 in a Swedish edition
entitled Filosofins Historia: Antiken och Medeltiden

© Anders Wedberg 1958

This translation © Bergljot Wedberg 1982

British Library Cataloguing in Publication Data
Wedberg, Anders
A history of philosophy.
Vol. 1: Antiquity and the Middle Ages
1. Philosophy—History
I. Title
ISBN 0-19-824639-0
0-19-824691-9 paperback

Library of Congress Cataloging in Publication Data
Wedberg, Anders, 1913–1978.
A history of philosophy.
Translation of: Filosofins historia.
Includes index.
Contents: v. 1. Antiquity and the Middle Ages.
1. Philosophy—History. I. Title.
B99.S82W413   190   81-22418
ISBN 0-19-824639-0   AACR2
0-19-824691-9 paperback

Typeset by Anne Joshua Associates, Oxford
Printed in Great Britain
at the University Press, Oxford
by Eric Buckley
Printer to the University

Note on the Translation

Several people have been involved in the translation into English of the present work. The translation of volumes I and II was begun by Mr John Swaffield. Volume III was first translated by Professor David E. Johnson. In the end, however, Wedberg himself embarked on a translation and produced a version that seems to be essentially his own work. Dr Mark Platts went over the whole of this version and had several discussions of it with Wedberg in 1973. The translation as it now appears is substantially the one Wedberg left behind when he died in 1978. Some polishing has been done by me and by Hans-Jörgen Ulfstedt (vol. I) and Torkel Franzén (vols. II and III) of the philosophy department, University of Stockholm, and by the staff of the Oxford University Press. The proofs were read by Torkel Franzén. Thanks are due to Professor J. L. Ackrill, Professor of the History of Philosophy in the University of Oxford, for his assistance in the preparation of the English edition.

Dag Prawitz

Contents

x *Contents*

Introduction

Even though the development of ideas traditionally known as the history of philosophy is only a narrow current in the broad stream of human culture through the centuries, it is still too rich to admit a comprehensive view. In writing history, some principle of selection must always be decided on. This also applies to the history of philosophy.

A selection, presumably without any guiding principle, has already been made by time itself. Of the literature of ancient philosophy only fragments have been preserved. Often we know nothing of the contents of those books that have disappeared. For this reason no one will ever be able to write an account of what really went on in ancient philosophy that does full justice to those involved.

Even when original sources are available, external circumstances impose a selection which is also very likely to be unsystematic. The enormous mass of extant medieval literature is for the most part scattered in manuscript form among the various libraries of Europe. No one today has a comprehensive view of what is actually written in this literature, and many generations are likely to pass before the situation substantially improves.

The more recent European philosophical literature is preserved in print, without any very important exceptions. It, too, is so copious, however, that no one is thoroughly familiar with all of it .

It is an intriguing and also a disturbing thought that if none of the relevant historical facts were forgotten or inaccessible, the history of philosophy would perhaps be very different from what it is usually made out to be. Many of the philosophers who today appear as great and original thinkers may in fact only have had a talent for giving striking expression to ideas that should be credited to unknown forerunners. And many philosophers who are unknown to us, or seldom given a thought, may belong among the great names. Indeed we can be quite sure that this is so. For we have already seen the appearance of many radical and soundly motivated re-evaluations. The numerous pioneers of the nineteenth century in the field of logic and in the more exact branches of philosophy have only recently been given their due by historians of philosophy. Often a temporarily victorious school of thought has belittled its vanquished or superseded opponents, and this negative evaluation has then in many cases gone uncontested for centuries. Since Galileo, Descartes, and others of the seventeenth century condemned medieval Scholasticism—to choose but one example out of many—a one-sidedly negative view of it has prevailed, until in our own time it has come to be realized that Scholasticism was by no means inferior on all points to post-Scholastic philosophy.

In this history I shall confine myself exclusively to the Western philosophical tradition which began in Greece during antiquity, went on through medieval Christian philosophy, and has been continued in more recent times by the philosophy of the countries dominated by European culture. There is thus much that will be passed over in silence; above all, the Indian and Chinese philosophy which is independent of this Western tradition. Also, medieval Arabic and Jewish philosophy, two offshoots of the same tradition. My silence in these matters is mainly due to my ignorance of the subject.

However, even within these confines, and among the facts that are readily available, the historian of philosophy must make a further selection. Take at random a great philosopher, say Plato. He manifests himself in his writings as a fascinating and enormously complex personality. The man Plato is well worth studying. He was a brilliant author, master of many styles: he could present an abstract debate as a tense drama, he could depict a person with irony and respectful sympathy, he was a sharp-eyed observer of human behaviour, and he could present grandiose visions of existence with virtuosity. Plato was one of the great figures of world literature. He was both a theoretical and an impractically practising politician. Through his totalitarian views he holds a noteworthy place in the history of political ideologies. He was a mathematician and a theoretical astronomer, an analyst of concepts and a logician. In short, he held views on almost everything. All his views were more or less intimately connected with his central philosophical theory, the doctrine of Ideas. The doctrine is, in part, a kind of religion, and Plato was, in a sense, the founder of a religion, or rather a religious current, which was to merge with Christianity. All this is worth writing about. It should be added that on all points Plato has exercised a literally immeasurable influence on the development of ideas in the West. His historical role is also worth studying. In the same way, most of the great classical philosophers present very many interesting aspects. In what follows, however, I have concentrated my attention on the intellectual problems and theories of the philosophers. The reader who desires to become acquainted with the human beings who had these problems and theories must go elsewhere—likewise the reader who is interested in philosophy as literature or as a cultural force.

Without striving for strict consistency, I have above all tried to follow the evolution of such philosophical problems and theories as can be subsumed under the—admittedly rather general—headings of epistemology, philosophy of language, logic, philosophy of science. I have almost entirely neglected the following: first, such views as belong today to some well-established particular science (mathematics, physics, biology, history, etc.); second, all those views on morals, politics, aesthetics, etc., that have essentially expressed the philosopher's commitment to certain values or norms; and third, what I propose to call attempts to formulate "deep truths". Under this last, deliberately vague, designation I subsume such theories as Parmenides' doctrine of Being, Plato's doctrine of the external world of Ideas, the translation Christian philosophers have made of their faith into the language of intellectual argumentation, the grand metaphysical systems constructed by Spinoza, Leibniz, Fichte, Schelling, Hegel, Schopenhauer, and many others. In order not to be forced to disrupt the historical continuity too harshly, I have, however, frequently stepped outside my self-imposed boundaries.

It has often been pointed out that a verbal description of a historical development is, in several essentials, similar to a map. In order to make proper use of a map, one usually needs a set of instructions explaining the relation between the map and reality. The same holds for a historical account such as this, and I shall now endeavour to give a few brief instructions.

1. *The schematic mode of presentation.* I have throughout schematized the philosophical theories that I present. In its original version, a theory can be likened to a face delineated by a multitude of interlacing strokes or fine dashes; my presentation of the same theory is like a drawing which depicts the face by a few simple lines. It is almost always possible to discern in the original picture—the philosopher's own words—several competing faces. I have then seized upon the one that has interested me most. The reader will get a grossly erroneous idea of the philosophical writings I discuss unless he keeps in mind this, my method of projection.

2. *"Precisation"*. When giving an account of a philosophical theory, one can restrict oneself to a more or less faithful translation, or paraphrase, of the philosopher's own words. In many cases I have gone a step further. It is characteristic of many philosophical statements that they are to some extent ambiguous or indefinite. A formulation that is lacking in clarity can be made clearer in several different ways.

Borrowing the terminology of the Norwegian philosopher Arne Naess, we can say that the "precisation" of a formulation can be carried out along different paths and that one can go a longer or shorter way on each path. In Naess's terminology a formulation *A* is an "interpretation" of a formulation *B* if *A* and *B* can mean the same (for a person, relative to a linguistic usage, in a certain cultural environment, etc.). *B*, he says, is a "precisation" of *A* if the set of all interpretations of *B* is a proper subset of the set of all interpretations of *A*. To make a statement *A* "more precise" is thus to replace *A* by a statement *B* which is open to some of, but not all, the interpretations that *A* admits. In many cases I have suggested certain precisations, in this sense.

One might demand of a historical exposition such as the present one that the account it gives shall, as far as possible, have exactly the same degree of precision or lack of precision

as the ideas or writings presented. I think that this requirement would be unfortunate. I believe, e.g., that one understands Plato's own statements relating to the doctrine of
Ideas better if he has in mind a "precisation" such as the one
I shall state, and with the aid of which he can discern a
structure in Plato's reasoning.

3. *The possibility of alternative precisations.* What I have
just said implies that many philosophical theories which I
shall here interpret in a certain way, could, in my opinion,
with equal right be interpreted in other ways. In Plato's
dialogues one could seize upon other statements than those
that have particularly caught my attention. Even if a historian
based his account on the same statements as those I have
singled out, he could mould them into a different pattern.

4. *The two realities.* As a precisation of certain ideas in
pre-Socratic Greek philosophy I have formulated a proposition "H. The phenomena of nature are determined strictly
according to law." I expect that most of my readers will
more or less consciously refer this proposition to two
different realities. When they read H, they will take a stand,
more or less clearly, regarding two completely different
questions, namely: (a) How does the proposition correspond
to what the pre-Socratic Greek philosophers of nature really
thought? and (b) To what extent is the proposition H a
correct description of the world? Through the precisation
I have made question (a) more problematic, while—I hope
—making question (b) less difficult to answer. But here I
must warn the reader against another possible misunderstand-
ing. I have made certain views of the Greek philosophers
more precise with the help of H, but H itself could be made
more precise in many different ways. As long as the precisation has not been carried so far as to make further precisation impossible, question (b) does not have an absolutely
unequivocal answer. It would therefore be a mistake to think
that I have read into the views of the ancient philosophers
certain (absolutely) precise assertions which can be said
unequivocally to hold or not to hold of the world. An
attempt to attain absolute precision would not be feasible
within a historical exposition such as this, and would in many
cases be lacking in interest.

5. *Criticism.* My ambition has been to write an account in which not the philosophers themselves, but their ideas, come alive. I have also, in the case of most of the philosophers discussed, wanted to create a dialogue between the reader and the philosopher, so that not only an increased store of memorized facts in the field of the history of ideas will result from the reading, but also a certain amount of intellectual stimulation. My somewhat irreverent criticism of many of the great names in the history of philosophy is intended to create an atmosphere in which such a dialogue can take place.

6. *The reliability of the exposition.* Any attempt to sketch the history of philosophy is bound to be somewhat unreliable owing to the fact that part of the literature no longer exists, or is inaccessible, or else is so extensive that no one can survey it all. The personal degree of ignorance in the historian is an additional factor of uncertainty. While I believe myself to be fairly well read in the ancient and modern literature of philosophy, I wish to emphasize that my account of medieval philosophy is based on a first-hand knowledge of the sources which is limited, essentially, to such great names as Aquinas, Augustine, and Ockham. I have therefore in many cases relied on secondary sources for additional information.

ANTIQUITY

1. PERIODS AND TRENDS IN ANCIENT PHILOSOPHY

Thales of Miletus, who is said to have predicted a solar eclipse which occurred in the year 585 BC, is usually regarded as the first Greek philosopher. Since the words 'philosopher' and 'philosophy' are not precisely definable, there is a certain arbitrariness in this view. But one must begin somewhere, and this is the tradition I shall follow. Most of the philosophers who appeared in the world of Greek culture during the sixth and the first half of the fifth centuries were scientists just as much as philosophers. They gradually evolved a conception of the universe, fragmentary and often incorrect, but nevertheless containing many anticipations of ideas later presented by science. The greatest name in this tradition of natural philosophy was probably Democritus, the foremost representative of Greek atomic theory. These natural philosophers will be discussed under the heading The Elements and Laws of Nature (Chapter I).

While the natural philosophers created the intellectual background for natural science, mathematics was developed in Greece into a systematic, abstract science. In pure mathematics thought seems to arrive, by itself, independently of the senses, at truths of a kind different from those of natural science. A number of philosophers who played an active role in the development of mathematics, or who held mathematics to be the paradigm of knowledge, were thereby led to emphasize the difference between sensory knowledge and rational knowledge, as well as that between the material world and a postulated reality accessible only to thought. Notions such as these were combined with moral and religious notions of an antithesis between earthly human and divine reality. In Plato (427–347 BC), the most influential of these philosophers, ideas of this kind merged with his logico-semantic theory of general concepts, the so-called theory of Ideas. This trend of thought will be discussed under the heading Religion and Mathematics (Chapter II).

Aristotle (384–322 BC) was at first a follower of Plato. In time he disengaged himself from his teacher and strove, without complete success, to effect a synthesis of the rival claims of experience and thought. He laid the foundation for formal logic and worked out a methodology of the deductive sciences, but he also shared the natural philosophers' interest in investigating nature, and he created a framework of scientific concepts which has exerted an enormous influence far into modern times. Aristotle is the subject of a special chapter, The Methods of Science (Chapter III).

The early natural philosophers seem to have been scientifically naïve in the sense that they were interested in describing nature, but not, or only slightly, in analysing the terminological and intellectual instruments used in the description. The names Socrates, Plato, and Aristotle mark the stages in a development away from this *naïveté*. One of the many expressions of their reflection on scientific reflection was their interest in analysing and defining concepts. They can be considered the originators of the analytic trend in philosophy, which has come to play such a dominant role in our time. For a modern philosopher it is instructive to see how critical and uncritical, rational and irrational, moral and theoretical, motives combined in the birth of concept analysis. This is sketched under the heading Socratic Concept Analysis and Platonic–Aristotelian Speculation (Chapter IV).

Abstract logical research was initiated by Aristotle and then continued chiefly by the Stoics, who were otherwise mainly interested in advocating a view and manner of life. The technically complex character of the problems and theories formulated by the ancient logicians is the reason for taking up Ancient Logic in a chapter by itself (Chapter V).

As early as the fifth century there appeared in the Greek cities a kind of practical philosopher, the Sophist, whose contact with scientific investigation was often slight, and who was chiefly interested in problems pertaining to the wisdom and conduct of everyday life. The ancient philosophers after Aristotle, who came from all provinces of the Hellenistic world and often were not of Greek origin, were concerned primarily with man's place in the world, his relations with his fellow-men and the gods, and the best way to live one's life. The various schools of thought contended for souls in order to set them on their special roads to salvation. In this struggle they had powerful competitors in the many oriental religious sects which at the same time were gaining ground in the Greco-Roman world. In the end they were all defeated by one of these sects, Christianity, which in the fourth century AD was decreed the official religion of the Roman Empire. These philosophical trends will be presented very briefly in The Art of Living: Morals and Salvation (Chapter VI).

I

The Elements and Laws of Nature

2. PRE-GREEK AND GREEK SCIENCE

In the Egyptian and Mesopotamian civilizations some sciences had already attained a fairly high level several thousand years before Christ. This is especially true of astronomy, mathematics, and medicine. The Greek debt of gratitude to these civilizations was certainly great, even though historical research has not been able to define its extent. The earliest Greek philosophers knew scarcely more about the world than what was known long before in Egypt and Mesopotamia, and perhaps in other parts of Asia as well. Yet they represented something essentially new in the history of thought.

Theoretical science has one of its roots in the technical knowledge acquired in many fields of vital importance long before man had learned how to formulate scientific theories. Thus geometry had its origin in the practical skill of surveyors and builders. Chemistry developed from the experiences that craftsmen such as potters, glass blowers, moulders, and plasterers had gathered. The branch of mechanics that deals with the equilibrium of forces could take off from the methods used by merchants weighing their goods and by builders using levers. A theoretical science arises when people are no longer satisfied with rules of thumb, telling them what to do to get such and such a result, and so set up systems of general, logically interrelated propositions, most of them perhaps without immediate application. The historical transition from technique to theoretical science is not marked by any sharp boundary. Anyhow, it does appear that this passage was first made in earnest by the Greeks. If we may believe what they themselves have written about the history of their science, their first philosophers were pioneers in this respect.

In ancient Egypt and Mesopotamia scientific studies were

often associated with the temples and carried on by priests in their official capacities. These studies were undertaken for religious reasons as much as for their practical importance. For example, the heavenly bodies were considered to be divine beings influencing what happens on earth, and it was therefore imperative to pay close attention to their behaviour. Greek science, on the other hand, was pursued by thinkers who were motivated by personal curiosity, and often in opposition to traditional religion. The Babylonian astronomer held to mythological ideas about the nature of the heavenly bodies, while measuring their orbits in the sky with patience and great exactness. He did not fit his scientific findings into anything like a scientific view of the universe. In this respect also Greek science appears to have been a new start in the history of thought. The philosophers whose ideas we shall now become acquainted with helped to create an intelligible picture of the universe as a whole, a picture built upon experience and reflection, unfettered by religious traditions.

This is not the place to try to explain the factors in Greek culture that favoured this new mode of thought. They are usually credited to the political constitutions of the small Greek city states, the peculiarities of the Greek popular religion, its lack of firm organization and doctrinal system, and the Greeks' bustling contacts through shipping and trade with the different cultures around the Mediterranean basin.

3. THE PRIMARY SUBSTANCE: THE MILESIAN SCHOOL

The first names we meet in the history of Greek philosophy are Thales (*c.*624–546 BC), Anaximander (*c.*611–546 BC), and Anaximenes (who died *c.*525 BC). They all lived in the city of Miletus on the west coast of Asia Minor in the sixth century before Christ and are thought to have been related to each other as teacher to disciple, in the order given. All three of them posed the same question: "What is the origin (or beginning: *arche*) of all things?" or "What is the primary substance (*physis*) of which all things consist?" To this query each supplied his own answer. Thales said water: *hydor* (or what flows: *to hygron*), Anaximander said the infinite (or the indefinite: *to apeiron*), and Anaximenes said air (or wind,

vapour: *aer*). After 2,500 years we can only dimly comprehend the meaning of their question and their answers. It is
a priori credible that not only the choice but also the very
concept of primary substance changed during the three
generations in which the Milesian school flourished. It is
quite possible that the notion of an 'origin' or 'primary substance ' was less sophisticated in Thales' thought than in that
of Anaximander or Anaximenes, and that, hence, the position that Thales attributed to water was not quite the same as
the one that Anaximander gave to *apeiron* or Anaximenes
to air. But the incompleteness of our sources does not permit us to indicate with any certainty the differences that may
have occurred here between the three thinkers. With full
awareness of the fact that my interpretation—like any other
—is highly uncertain and ignores differences which must
have existed, I read the following ideas into the Milesian
doctrines.

A. Each thing has arisen from, and will return to, the
   primary substance.

The word *arche* means something like origin, beginning. Idea
A is perhaps the one we can most confidently ascribe to the
Milesian philosophers. Thales, who identified the primary
substance with water, no doubt thought about the origin and
disappearance of things by analogy with the many phenomena he could observe daily: fish and marine growth forming
in the sea and then disappearing, clouds arising from the
surface of the sea and being precipitated as rain, and so on.
All the Milesian philosophers were intensely interested in
"meteorological" phenomena which at that time were understood to include all that happened in the heavens, whether
in the atmosphere or in celestial space. Anaximenes, for
example, who identified the primary substance with air,
thought of the origin and disappearance of things in the same
way in which he interpreted meteorological phenomena:
wind, clouds, rain, the sun, the moon, and the stars; and
these he explained by his theory of the condensation and
rarefaction of air.

B. Everything is a portion of the primary substance in a
   certain qualitative state.

This interpretation, in itself admittedly very vague, of the theory of primary substance is supported by Aristotle's testimony. In the *Metaphysics* he says:

That of which all things that are consist, and from which they first came to be, and into which they are finally resolved—the substance remaining but changing in its modifications—this they [i.e. the earliest natural philosophers] say is the element and the principle of things, and therefore they think nothing is either generated or destroyed, since this nature is always conserved, as we say Socrates neither comes to be absolutely when he comes to be beautiful or musical, nor ceases to be when he loses these characteristics, because the substratum, Socrates himself, remains.[1]

Idea B gives a more precise shape to the theory stated in A. The generation of a thing means that a portion of the primary substance assumes a specific state, and its destruction that this same portion sheds that state. The same type of observations that inspired the Milesians to postulate A probably also constituted the empirical basis for B. It is, for example, an everyday experience that the same quantity of water can occur now as a fluid, now as ice, and now as steam. The same quantity of matter can thus be found existing sometimes in a water state, sometimes in an ice state, and sometimes in a steam state. Given the boldness to generalize that the Milesian philosophers possessed, it was easy to pass from such observations to the theory that all differences between things are merely differences in the state of a single substance.

Ideas A and B together imply:

C. The primary substance can occur either in its undifferentiated primary state—as water (Thales), as *apeiron* (Anaximander), as air (Anaximenes)—or in one or another differentiated thing state.

When an object arises from the primary substance, say Anaximenes' air, according to B a certain quantity of the substance changes from its primary state, the air state, into something else.

We come, I think, one step closer to the unattainable ideal of a full understanding of the Milesian doctrines if we also take into consideration the following idea:

---

[1] Aristotle, *Metaphysics*, I 3, 983[b].

D. Any quantity of the primary substance can, under suitable circumstances, assume any differentiated thing state whatsoever.

This idea is a natural completion of, not to say conclusion from, ideas A and B. Assume that a differentiated thing exists at a certain moment of time. According to A it will at some time disappear into the primary substance; but from the primary substance, according to A, everything originates. Surely no part of the primary substance has greater possibilities for development than any other part, apart from purely quantitative considerations.

Idea D could be used in turn as an argument for A and B. This was done by Diogenes of Apollonia, a fifth-century follower of Anaximenes' opinion that the primary substance is air. Diogenes says:

In my view all things are, in a word, variations of one and the same. It is all one and the same thing. This is obvious. For if of the things that are now found in this world (earth and water and air and fire and everything else that occurs in the world), one thing were distinct in nature from another, and if it [the primary substance] did not remain the same under its many transformations and modifications, then things could in no way combine together and be of any use or harm to each other. No plant could spring from the ground, and animals and other things could not come into existence if things were not so constituted that they are one and the same thing. But all these things are merely variations of the same; they assume sometimes one, sometimes another, form and return at last to the same.[2]

We do not know whether Thales had already elaborated the idea of a primary substance so as to arrive at D. In most of Greek thought on matters of natural philosophy, the idea of certain basic pairs of opposites played an important part. The pairs of opposites that most often recur are wet and dry, and cold and warm. But many others, dark and light, big and small, etc., are important for one thinker or another. Anaximander seems to have considered the transformation of the primary substance as coalescence and separation of such opposites. Anaximenes had the most advanced theory

[2] H. Diels, *Die Fragmente der Vorsokratiker* (7th edn., Berlin: Weidmannsche Verlagsbuchhandlung, 1954), 64 B 2.

on this question. According to him the transformation of matter always involves a condensation or rarefaction of the primary substance. Each subsequent member of the series of fire–air–wind–clouds–water–earth–stone is, on his view, a condensation of the preceding member.

The doctrine of the four elements, earth, water, air, and fire, is associated especially with a later thinker, Empedocles. In his conception of nature they received a role they had not played before. But long before Empedocles' time these four had apparently been objects of special attention. All four occur in the sequence of states mentioned above, which Anaximenes postulated. The idea that they are major successive stages in the transformations of the primary substance seems to have been quite common. The Greek philosophers may perhaps have been inspired here by a time-honoured and widespread stock of ideas. Herodotus tells of the Persians that they used to ascend to the highest peaks of the mountains and offer sacrifices to Zeus, "calling the whole vault of the sky Zeus", and also to "sun, moon, earth, fire, water, and winds". In the Chandogya Upanishads, fire, water, earth, winds, and space are stated to be the elements of the world.[3]

Why did Thales characterize the primary element just as water, and Anaximenes just as air? If a given quantity of the primary element can appear as either earth or water or air or fire or something else, in what sense then did Thales say that it "is" water, and Anaximenes that it "is" air? It is impossible to reply to this question with any certainty. Reminiscences of religious myths of creation may, as Aristotle intimates, have inspired Thales. Otherwise, what probably contributed to the privileged position of water in the universe of Thales was that there was so much of it. It has been suggested (by Pierre Duhem) that Thales' view of the universe was similar to that of Genesis in the Bible, i.e. that he thought of it as a hemispherical bubble at whose bottom the earth floats, and under whose roof the stars travel; above the heavens is water, and below the earth is water. Similarly, Anaximander taught that *apeiron* contains within itself all the worlds in the universe. Air played the same dominant role

[3] *Encyclopedia of Religion and Ethics*, ed. James Hastings, Vol. II, Edinburgh–New York, 1909.

in Anaximenes' universe; this is an ocean of air in which the heavenly bodies float. The idea of an unfilled or empty space was foreign to the Milesian philosophers—the Atomists were the first to uphold it. As an item of the Milesian theory we can therefore, with a fair degree of assurance, state the doctrine:

E. The primary substance fills the entire universe, mostly in its undifferentiated primary state.

If we can believe the neo-Platonist Simplicius (AD 500), Anaximander described the primary substance as *apeiron* (the infinite, the indefinite) simply because, contrary to the other two Milesians, he found it arbitrary to identify the primary substance with any of the states in which it can occur.

Many of the notions that have now been presented bear witness to how little the Milesians knew of the physical universe, and yet how daringly they speculated upon it. But the doctrine of the primary substance, especially the ideas B and D, can also be considered as a remarkable anticipation of our modern theories on the nature of matter. We know today that everything is not really water or air. But just as the Milesians did, we too assume that matter is ultimately far more homogeneous than it appears to immediate observation. A moment's reflection also shows that with their theory of a primary substance, the Milesian philosophers—whether they were blessed with prophetic intuition or not, and independently of how ignorant they were of facts now known— pointed to a method for the scientific understanding of the world. One may also say that their theories were stimulating, albeit vague and incorrect, working hypotheses. If we assume that everything reduces to one and the same primary substance, we can draw a number of important conclusions.

F. All phenomena are fundamentally similar.

The heavenly phenomena—the weather and the stars—no longer have any mysterious divine character, but are in principle of the same nature as the things we meet on the surface of the earth. The Milesians' strong meteorological interest caused them to apply their theory of the transformations of the primary substance first and foremost to the heavenly phenomena. Living beings are also, on their theory, essentially similar to inorganic things. The Milesians conceived of the soul, not in the light of the confusing experience of religious ecstasy, but as one of the forms in which the primary substance appears.

If all phenomena are fundamentally similar, it follows further:

G. The as yet unexplained can be explained by analogy with the well-known.

If, with Thales, we assume that everything is water, then it is only natural to think that by studying how the water around us behaves we can arrive at the secrets of more mysterious phenomena. This is what Thales did. Here is an example. Accepting the idea common to the Mediterranean peoples of antiquity, that the solid ground is everywhere surrounded by water, he enquired into the cause of earthquakes. A piece of wood that floats on the sea rocks when it meets a wave. According to Thales, earthquakes can be explained in the same way: the earth floats upon the oceans, and when the waves raise it, earthquakes occur. With his theory of the condensation and rarefaction of air, Anaximenes tried to explain meteorological phenomena such as winds, clouds, thunder, snow and rainbows. We know today that the Milesians' explanations by analogy were largely incorrect. But our explanations differ from theirs not so much in the method by which they have been obtained, as in the fact that we have an incomparably richer experience to draw upon.

H. The phenomena of nature are determined strictly according to law.

If everything "is" water or *apeiron* or air, then all things must be subject to the laws of the behaviour of just water or *apeiron* or air. Thales and his followers did not express themselves in this abstract manner, but, as we have seen, their reasonings conformed to this pattern. From here it was only another step to the idea that all occurrences in nature are subject to general laws. Anaximander was the one who came closest to an explicit formulation of this view. He apparently thought that there is a law according to which things at their proper times arise from, and then return to, *apeiron*, a law he considered analogous to the law by which a judge tries a criminal.

I.   Matter is constant

The origin and annihilation of things that we see about us each day signifies merely that parts of the primary substance are being transformed from one state to another.

J.   The universe has neither a beginning nor an end in time.

The primary substance itself persists from eternity to eternity, and thus the universe as well, being filled with the primary substance.

K.   The "world" that now surrounds us—the earth, the oceans, the living beings, the celestial bodies—has originated not through any divine act of creation, but through long-lasting processes of the same kind as those that are steadily going on around us.

Anaximander believed that the basic opposites were once separated out from *apeiron*. The earth was then formed in the centre of the universe, and at first was entirely covered by the sea. Above the sea the air-space and the celestial bodies were separated off. The latter, he thought, are rings filled with fire which pours out through holes in them. Because of the heat of the sun, a steady vaporization of the sea takes place, a vaporization which is the cause of the earth's dry crust here and there coming to light and which will eventually lead to the complete drying out of the entire earth. Living beings originated in the warm slime of the sea, and man is descended from the fish. Anaximenes thought that the earth and the celestial bodies came into existence through condensations in the original sea of air, and that they now hover above us somewhat like thin discs—therefore they do not fall down.

L.   The multiplicity of worlds in an infinite cosmos.

Both Anaximander and Anaximenes are reported to have put forward the hypothesis that the "world" in which we find ourselves—roughly, our earth with the planets and the sphere of fixed stars—will some day disintegrate just as it was one day formed, and that the formation and disintegration of such worlds is a phenomenon that periodically repeats itself in infinity. Anaximander is also supposed to have taught that in the cosmos there are an infinite number of simultaneously existing worlds similar to ours, and that worlds are forming and disintegrating continually.

The Milesians were not materialists in the modern understanding of this term, simply because they did not have the modern, say post-Cartesian, notion of matter. They knew of no clear separation between matter and force, nor between matter and mind. Thales is reported as having said that the magnet attracts the iron by its "soul", and that everything is full of gods.[4] Anaximander is said to have looked upon *apeiron* as divine and as that which rules everything.[5] Anaximenes is reported to have identified the air with God, and one of his utterances was: "As our soul, which is air, rules us, so also do breath and air contain the whole universe."[6]

4. NATURAL PHILOSOPHY AND VIEWS OF LIFE: XENOPHANES AND HERACLITUS

The ideas that have come down to us from the Milesian philosophers give expression to a world view which cannot but speak to our feelings. The effect on us, having tasted so many ways of seeing the world, can be at most a pale reflection of the emotional loading this view must have carried in Greece in the sixth century BC. On the whole, the earliest Milesian philosophers speak, in preserved fragments and commentaries, with the objective voice of the investigator. But in many later Greek philosophers the implications of natural philosophy for man's attitude toward life are very strongly brought out.

Xenophanes was born in the city of Colophon on the west coast of Asia Minor about the middle of the sixth century BC, but emigrated to the Greek colony of Elea in the south west of Italy. He is supposed to have been a pupil of Anaximander. His contributions as a scientist seem to

---

[4] Diels, *Die Fragmente der Vorsokratiker*, 11 A 22.
[5] Ibid. 12 A 15.   [6] Ibid. 13 A 10, 13 B 2.

have been unimportant, but he gave open expression to the
criticism of traditional religious beliefs to which the Milesian
conception of nature must necessarily lead. The pious rever-
ence bestowed by the folk religion on its gods he transferred
to the law-bound universe itself. "God" was for him the same
as the "cosmos" or the eternal order of things. He spoke
sarcastically of the gods of Greek mythology: "If cattle,
horses, or lions had hands and could paint and shape the
works of men, then horses would paint equine, and cattle
bovine, gods and produce such forms as they themselves
possess."[7]

Heraclitus lived in the city of Ephesus on the west coast
of Asia Minor about 500 BC. His new answer to the old
question of the Milesians was to say that fire is the primary
substance. His interest in natural science seems to have been
slight, and he stood closer to traditional religion than the
Milesians did. In oracular utterances which won him the
epithet, "the Obscure", he expresses a sense and evaluation
of life which religion and the Milesian ideas of nature inspired
in him. The idea of a primary substance can be experienced
intellectually in at least two different ways. One can hold fast
to the notion that the same matter persists through all transformations, and thus experience that there is constancy and
stability behind the restless change in the world. Or one can
focus attention on the idea that even the apparently most
stable things are only temporary forms of the ever-changing
primary substance—forms it will soon discard—and thus
be led to a sense of the inconstancy of all things. Most of the
Greek philosophers stressed the first aspect of the theory of
primary substance; what they emphasized was that there is
no real origin or destruction in nature. But in Heraclitus we
meet an overwhelmingly strong reaction of the second kind.
He expressed his view in assertions such as:

Who steps into the same river, to him there ever flow other waters.[8]

It is impossible to step twice into the same river.[9]

All things come into being by conflict of opposites, and the sum of
all things flows like a stream.[10]

---

[7] Ibid. 21 B 15.   [8] Ibid. 22 B 12.
[9] Ibid. 22 B 91.   [10] Diogenes Laertius, IX 8.

His view was summarized by later ancient writers in the famous formula, "Everything flows" (*panta rhei*).

In Heraclitus' universe there is also something that he feels to be permanent and indestructible. But it is hardly matter, the primary substance, but rather the eternal law according to which change takes place, a law which is fate and necessity. Change implies that opposite qualities drive each other out.

Cold becomes warm, warm cold; wet dry, dry wet.[11]

Fire lives the death of earth, and air lives the death of fire; water lives the death of air, earth that of water.[12]

(The reference to air in the last quotation is perhaps a later Stoic addition to Heraclitus' original saying.) It appears that Heraclitus assumed the transformation of fire to occur as shown in diagram (A).

(A)

In this connection, Heraclitus spoke of the downward and the upward roads, and this most probably not in a merely figurative sense: the blue sky was often held by the Greeks of his time to be of a fiery nature. He claimed the two roads to be the same, presumably in the sense that transformations in the opposite directions are taking place simultaneously, always and everywhere. The stability which seems to characterize so much of our world means only that transformations in opposite directions balance each other.

Periodically, however, this balance is disturbed; fire takes the upper hand and the entire world is destroyed. But each time, after a while, a new world rises again. Heraclitus is thus one of the first Greek representatives of the view, so common in antiquity, that the history of the universe is periodic. It is later found in Empedocles, Plato, and Aristotle, in the Stoics and the neo-Platonists. The periodicity could be thought to

---

[11] Diels, *Die Fragmente der Vorsokratiker*, 22 B 126.
[12] Ibid. 22 B 76.

affect a smaller or a larger number of features. When, as sometimes happened, the periodicity was believed to concern everything without exception, the view became a doctrine of a strict, eternal recurrence. The periodicity was conceived on analogy with the periodicity of the seasons of the year, and the period itself was often referred to as "the great year". Heraclitus is credited with the opinion that the length of the great year was 18,000 years.

The soul of man is akin to the universal fire. The more fiery, the drier and warmer the soul is, the more noble and reasonable it is, too. The universal fire itself is besouled, and Heraclitus gives it the name "God".

For the uneducated masses and for philosophical colleagues who did not perceive these truths, Heraclitus harboured the most heart-felt contempt.

Heraclitus' paradox of the thing undergoing change, which both *is* and *is not* the same thing, still has a certain theoretical interest. It points to the fact that a changing object can be considered as a series of successive, mutually non-identical states. It also raises the question: by what principle—or principles—do we count states at different times as states of the same object? In modern philosophy it is sometimes said that two states that are parts of the history of the same object are "genidentical". Genidentity is a relation different from strict identity. Problems concerning genidentity can with a certain historical right be considered as aspects of what could be called the Heraclitean problem.

5. MECHANISTIC NATURE AND SPIRIT: EMPEDOCLES AND ANAXAGORAS

The natural philosophers with whom we have become acquainted so far saw in nature a unified system ruled by law. In Greek philosophy another way of regarding the world appeared early on: a spiritual reality was thought to exist along with the material. Empedocles and Anaxagoras are two thinkers who essentially belong to the philosophical tradition inaugurated by Thales, but in whom we find the beginnings of this other outlook. They were both born at the beginning of the fifth century and were active at the same time, although in different parts of the Greek world: Empedocles in Sicily and southern Italy, Anaxagoras on the west coast of Asia Minor and in Athens. Anaxagoras developed his philosophy somewhat later than Empedocles, and there is evidence that he was influenced by, and consciously disputed, Empedocles' ideas.

A. *Common Ideas*

The two philosophers had in common a number of views which involve an important development of the Milesian theory of primary substance. The Milesians supposed that their primary substance filled the entire universe. If we define void as space in which there is no matter, it follows that there was no void in the Milesian universe. There is no evidence that the Milesians themselves stated this conclusion, but Empedocles and Anaxagoras did. "In all the cosmos there is no space that is empty, and neither is there any that is overfilled," said Empedocles.[13] The proposition:

(1) There is no void,

which was thus introduced into philosophical debate, has since had a long and intensive history. It was destined to be rejected by the Atomists, but defended by Aristotle, and because of his authority it persisted until the seventeenth and eighteenth centuries, when it was finally opposed by an equally powerful authority, Newtonian mechanics.

Empedocles and Anaxagoras assumed, like the Milesians, that there is no real origin or destruction. On the question of the constancy of matter they went a step further than the earlier theorists of a primary substance. The Milesians, and Heraclitus as well, supposed that the primary substance can change its qualities and appear sometimes as earth, sometimes as water, and so on. Empedocles, seconded by Anaxagoras, contested this theory and asserted:

(2) Matter is qualitatively unchangeable.

It is usually thought that this idea was inspired by the theory of the Italian philosopher, Parmenides, and that it constituted an attempt to fulfil as far as possible his demand for permanency, without condemning, as he did, the fleeting world of the senses as a mere illusion.

[13] Ibid. 31 B 13.

In opposition to their predecessors the two thinkers assumed:

(3) There is a plurality of primary substances.

Empedocles thought there were exactly four—earth, water, air, and fire—whereas Anaxagoras believed the number to be very large, if not infinite.
  Both supposed moreover:

(4) The apparent origin and destruction of matter is only the mixture and the separation of primary substances.

Mixture results in the origin of composite things, whereas the separation leads to their destruction.
  Still another common assumption was:

(5) The characteristics of a composite object are essentially dependent on the proportions in which the primary substances occur in it.

Ideas (2) to (5) can be considered as a first attempt towards the mechanization of the world picture that the Atomists were later to complete. Possibly Empedocles and Anaxagoras also thought that their primary substances appear in the form of certain very small homogeneous particles, and if so, they anticipated the Atomists on this point as well. On Anaxagoras' part at least, the evidence of the sources is so complex and uncertain, however, that it is impossible to ascribe to him with any conviction the assumption of such particles. More on this soon.

B. *Empedocles*

So much for their common theoretical background. Empedocles is the author of the famous doctrine of the four primary substances or four elements: earth, water, air, and fire, a doctrine which was later adopted and elaborated by Plato and by Aristotle.
  Of the ancient natural philosophers, Empedocles is one of the most versatile and also most difficult to understand. In his doctrine of the four elements he gave a new twist to an old idea. As a scientist he displayed brilliant intuition: for example, in asserting that light is transmitted at finite

speed. His theory of biological evolution is a primitive anticipation of Darwin. First the individual parts of living creatures appeared in isolation from one another; then they were united at random into weirdly mixed beings, creatures with the bodies of deer and the heads of men, for example. The present species have come about through a sort of natural selection.

In his cosmogony Empedocles spoke of two great forces, Love, by which the elements attract each other, and Hate, through which each element repels the other. Love is the good force, Hate the evil. They are engaged in an eternal struggle in which they alternately carry off the victory. The universe evolves in periodic fashion (see diagram (B)).

(B)

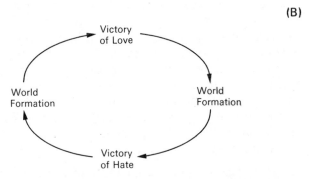

When Love is victorious, an immense sphere, the *sphairos*, is formed where the elements are so thoroughly blended that their specific characteristics are obliterated. After the influence of Hate has recommenced, the elements are then gradually separated out. In the course of this process, a world such as the one we know arises, only to disappear again as Hate progresses toward its complete victory. Worlds exist only when the two forces somehow balance each other.

In Empedocles the scientist and the moral and religious prophet were united. He taught that the body is merely foreign clothing worn temporarily by the soul. He also believed in the transmigration of souls. Evil souls must wander from body to body in punishment and endure the travails of life before they may return to bliss: "I have already once been a boy, a girl, a plant, a bird, and a mute fish leaping from the sea."[14] These ideas are not in the spirit of Milesian philosophy; they are similar to the almost contemporary views of the Pythagoreans, and they are a harbinger of Platonic dualism.

C. *Anaxagoras*

Anaxagoras postulated a very great, perhaps an infinite, number of primary substances. From the extant fragments we get the impression that he made a primary substance out of each of the classical opposites of the natural philosophers: wet and dry, cold and warm, dark and light, etc. Aristotle ascribes to him also the theory that there is a primary flesh substance, hair substance, gold substance, and so on. Anaxagoras is supposed to have expressly denied, however, that earth or water or air or fire are primary substances. If we can believe Aristotle, it would seem that Anaxagoras postulated a primary substance for every apparently homogeneous substance except for those very substances that Empedocles chose as his four elements. As for the number and choice of the primary substances, Anaxagoras makes a more primitive impression than his predecessor does. Let us, however, with an appearance of exactness, record the following as one of his doctrines:

(a) There is a large number of primary substances: E_1, E_2, E_3. . . .

He also asserted that "in everything there is a part of everything."[15] When a piece of matter is said to "be" flesh, or gold, or something of the kind, this does not mean that it consists exclusively of the primary flesh substance, or the primary gold substance, or any other primary substance. It means only that one particular primary substance is the dominant constituent of that piece. We may thus further discern the following assumptions in Anaxagoras' theory:

(b) Every primary substance enters into "everything".

(c) That a piece of matter "is" E_1, signifies merely that E_1 dominates the other primary substances therein.

---

[14] Ibid. 31 B 117.   [15] Ibid. 59 B 6, 11, 12.

Anaxagoras' reason for (b), and thus for (c), was apparently that, on his view, everything can develop out of anything, but that a primary substance cannot evolve from something that does not already contain it.

Assertion (b) is difficult to understand. One might suppose that Anaxagoras intended (b) to hold only for such pieces or portions of matter as are large enough to be seen, or touched, or in some other way apprehended with our senses. One might take him to mean merely that every primary substance is represented in each such sufficiently large quantity of matter. Aristotle's and other ancient authors' talk of "homogeneous things" (*homoiomere, homoiomereia*) in connection with Anaxagoras' theory could be interpreted as meaning that Anaxagoras thought every primary substance to be represented by certain particles which consist exclusively of this primary substance, and that every sufficiently large quantity of matter contains such particles of every primary substance.

This interpretation does not agree, however, with other views which can be attributed to Anaxagoras with great certainty:

(d) Every piece of matter is infinitely divisible, and by division all the parts can be made arbitrarily small.

(e) In every piece of matter, however small, each primary substance is present.

Clearly (e) excludes the existence of homogeneous particles in the sense just mentioned. On this point, too, Anaxagoras must have been of another opinion than Empedocles, who supposed each element to be represented by homogeneous (even if not indivisible) masses, i.e. masses that consist exclusively of the element in question.

How, then, should Anaxogoras' assumptions (b) and (c) be interpreted? In one of the fragments that have come down to us, he speaks of a mixture of infinitely small portions of the elements. If we take these infinitely small portions to be mere points, and if we consider the basic elements as properties not merely of bodies but also of points, thesis (b) could be interpreted thus:

(b′) Take any portion of matter, however small, and any basic property, then the portion contains a point having the property.

Many other interpretations could be advanced to satisfy the weak demand of giving a logically consistent meaning to Anaxagoras' statements. Unfortunately, the sources are so fragmentary that a reliable choice from among the various possibilities is impossible. If we could bring Anaxagoras back to life and ask him which of the interpretations he would be prepared to accept, it is only too likely that he would be unable to reply.[16]

Anaxagoras is supposed to have postulated an initial state when the primary substances were everywhere uniformly mixed. At a certain point in this uniform cosmos a turbulent motion arose as the result of the intervention of the "Spirit" (or "Reason"). This motion spread more and more until it led to the differentiation the universe now exhibits. The circular motions of the celestial bodies are an effect of it. Empedocles was wrong, however, when he postulated a periodic world formation and dissolution. The vortex motion initiated by the Spirit is a non-recurring phenomenon.

---

[16] When we seek a logically consistent interpretation of assumption (b), an appropriate alternative starting-point would be to understand his primary substances as basic properties of matter (but not of points). We can also suppose that each such property can be present in different degrees in different pieces of matter—from zero degrees, when the property is absent, on up. With these two points of departure, the following interpretations of (b) could be advanced.

(b²) Each basic property (primary substance) E_i is present to some positive degree in every piece of matter.

Another interpretation is:

(b³) If a piece of matter has the basic property E_i in zero degree, then this piece has a part which has E_i to a positive degree.

Still another interpretation is:

(b⁴) All macroscopic things consist of certain minute elementary particles of such a kind that each basic property of E_i is present to some positive degree in each part of the particle.

In the text we understood the concept of "homogeneous particle" in accordance with the following definition:

(D) x is a homogeneous particle = Df every part of x has only a single basic property.

If we substitute for this the following definition:

(D′) x is a homogeneous particle = Df each part of x has every basic property to the same degree as x,

then interpretation (b⁴) would be compatible with the expositions of Anaxagoras' theory by Aristotle and some other ancient authors.

Aristotle commends Anaxagoras for introducing the Spirit into his system, but complains that he did not use it systematically enough: the Spirit is allowed only to set the universal machinery in motion and now and then to intervene when Anaxagoras does not know the cause of some phenomenon. Plato, too, reproaches Anaxagoras for the same shortcoming.

Anaxagoras, who was born in Asia Minor, went to Athens during the reign of Pericles, and was the first to teach natural philosophy there. His opinion that the sun is a glowing mass of stone drew down upon him the accusation of godlessness from the pious of the city. The threat of the death penalty forced him to flee back to Asia Minor. This was probably the first in the long series of conflicts between free thinking and traditional religion.

6. ATOMS AND THE VOID: THE ATOMISTS

Greek natural philosophy reached its zenith with the atomistic theory, which was first set forth by Leucippus in the fifth century and perfected around the year 400 by Democritus, both of them from the Thracian city of Abdera. In the latter half of the fourth century their theory was adopted, with certain changes, by Epicurus. His system gained wide acceptance among the educated classes just before and after the birth of Christ. Ancient atomism is a brilliant conjecture which not only anticipated, but, when the time was ripe, also contributed to evoking the classical Galilean–Newtonian conception of physics. The so-called mechanistic view of the universe which philosophers and physicists developed in the seventeenth century and which came to dominate Western ideas of nature until the end of the nineteenth century was also in essential respects a revival of the hypothesis of the Atomists. This hypothesis appears even more ingenious when we remember that the ancient Atomists had only their everyday observations of nature to build upon. Their conjectures can be summarized under several headings as follows:

A. *The atomic structure of matter*

The material phenomena, in the widest meaning of the term, which we perceive with our senses are, apparently at least, of the most variegated nature. A stone, a liquid, a gas, a wave, a beam of light, a rainbow, a reflection, etc. have little in common to the immediate observer. Even if one were to stumble on the idea that such different phenomena are somehow of a similar nature, and then attempted to pick out one of them as fundamental, it is surely not at all clear which of them should be selected. The Atomists hit upon the idea that the pebble offers us the truest picture of the ultimate, imperceptible essence of matter. More specifically, they supposed that matter consists of certain very small, solid particles which are physically indivisible. (Epicurus held that each atom is composed of some finite number of minimal "points", the number being the measure of the size of the atom, but these points are, on his view, inseparably cemented together within the atom.) Because of this physical indivisibility, the particles were given the name "atoms". The Atomists attributed constancy to the particles in several respects: each atom has a constant size, a constant form, and, at least for the Epicureans, a constant weight.

B. *The homogeneity of matter*

Matter is homogeneous in the sense that the only properties that distinguish one atom from another, except for position and state of motion, are its form and size. This homogeneity finds an expression in the fact that what would today be called the specific weight is everywhere the same. The weight of the atoms is uniquely determined by their volume, and the weight of a composite object is the sum of the weights of the atoms it contains. In keeping with this view the Atomists also thought that the atoms are all alike inside: they are all completely solid; none is like a Swiss cheese with enclosed holes.

C. *The kinds of atom*

The homogeneity of matter does not rule out the existence of different kinds of atom, characterized by different shapes and sizes. All atoms are so small that we cannot perceive them with our senses, but within the atomic order of magnitude there is room for variety. Some atoms are round and smooth, some are rough, and some have hooks and projections. Let us say that two atoms are of the same kind if they have the same size and shape. According to some sources, Democritus thought that there are an infinite number of types of atom. According to the Epicureans, on the other hand, the infinite number of atoms in existence are distributed among only a finite number of kinds, there being an infinite number of atoms of each kind.

D. *The infinite number of atoms*

All the ancient Atomists seem to have been agreed that the number of atoms in the universe is infinite. Among the Epicureans, this thought was closely associated with the idea of the infinity of space; a finite number of atoms would be completely dispersed in infinite space.

E. *The constancy of matter*

The Milesian theory of a primary substance already contained the idea that this substance remains constant under all its changes of state. The Atomists gave the constancy of matter a more precise formulation: every atom, with its constant size and shape, exists eternally. None has ever come into being, and none will ever cease to exist. What we call the origin and destruction of things is merely the union and separation of atoms.

F. *The combinations of atoms*

Our modern ideas of attracting and repelling forces were foreign to the Atomists. Thus, they could not conceive of the combination of atoms into complicated structures other than in a crudely mechanistic way; because of their irregular shapes the atoms literally hook themselves onto each other. The apparent stability that characterizes so many objects about us is not duplicated, however, by similarly stable atomic connections. In the life of an atom motion is the normal thing.

The ancient Atomists made certain vague gropings towards a kind of chemical valence and molecular theory. According to Democritus not every atom can combine with any other atom; and the Epicureans thought that atoms first associate in certain primary groups, which may then be combined in groups of a higher order.

G. *The existence of the void*

All the primary-substance theoreticians seem to have assumed that the universe is everywhere filled with matter, and Empedocles and Anaxagoras explicitly denied the existence of a void. It was the Atomists who first assumed the existence of space not occupied by matter, by atoms. The void and the atoms are on an equal standing as constituents of their universe. In contrast to the void, the atoms were called "the full", "the solid", "the hard". Sometimes the contrast was described as one between "the existent" and "the nonexistent", a description which must not be construed to imply that there is no void.

H. *Absolute space*

The distinction between absolute and relative space, which plays a fundamental part in Newton's own exposition of his mechanics, was formulated by him as follows:

Absolute space, in its own nature, without relation to anything external, remains always similar and immovable. Relative space is some movable dimension or measure of the absolute spaces which our senses determine by its position to our bodies and which is commonly taken for immovable space; such is the dimension of a subterraneous, an aerial or celestial space, determined by its position in respect of the earth. Absolute and relative space are the same in figure and magnitude, but they do not remain always numerically the same. For if the earth, for instance, moves a space of our air, which relatively and in respect of the earth remains always the same, it will at one time be one part of the absolute space into which the air passes; at another time it will be another part of the same, and so, absolutely understood, it will be continually changed.[17]

Although the ancient Atomists never expressed themselves in such clear terms, one may, I think, attribute to them an intuitive conception of space which agrees with Newton's.

The fact that they considered space as a constituent of reality on a par with bodies (atoms) already seems to be evidence for this interpretation. The Epicurean doctrine of the fall of the atoms is further evidence. If the existence of

---

[17] H. S. Thayer (ed.), *Newton's Philosophy of Nature* (New York: Hafner 1953), pp. 17–18.

an absolute space, in Newton's sense, is postulated, then a "possible world" can be described in which all bodies maintain their relative positions, yet in which the entire system of bodies moves through absolute space, for example, at a constant velocity. If the existence of an absolute space is not assumed, such a description is impossible. The "possible world" thus described was assumed to be not only possible but actual (though in the past) by Epicurus and his school. According to the Epicurean theory this possible world coincides with the original state of the universe, in which all atoms were falling through space in parallel lines at a constant common speed. (The statements of this doctrine, e.g. by Lucretius in *De rerum natura*, are, however, difficult to interpret.)

I. *Time is not on a par with space*

Newton, who postulated absolute space, also postulated absolute time. For him absolute time was a constituent of reality on a par with absolute space. The ancient Atomists had a different notion. They declared that the two "elements" of reality are the atoms and the void (space), or that only these two "exist". They did not recognize time as a third element.

This view seems to have been so obvious to the first Atomists, Leucippus and Democritus, that they saw no need to argue for it—unless their definition of time as a "day-and-night-like" idea was intended as such. According to Epicurus, time is a kind of accident (roughly in the Aristotelian sense, cf. § 28). In the first book of *De rerum natura*, Lucretius very clearly presents this Epicurean conception. After formulating the orthodox two-element theory, he goes on to assert that everything else that can be mentioned at all is either a property or an accident of the two elements:

Time likewise exists not of itself, but only from actual things is derived the sense of what has been done in the past, then what thing is present with us, further what is to follow after. Nor may we admit that anyone has a sense of time by itself separated from the movement of things and quiet calm.[18]

[18] Lucretius, *De rerum natura*, I 459–63.

The atomistic view of time can be looked upon as an anticipation of the relative conception of time which was first clearly formulated by Leibniz in the seventeenth century. The Atomists thus occupy an interesting middle position between Newton, who held time as well as space to be absolute, and Leibniz, who took them both to be relative.

J. *The infinitude of space and time*

The Atomists taught that space as well as time is infinite. Democritus said that time is "eternal", and he apparently thought of time's eternity in such a way that time could be represented by an infinite straight line (see diagram (C)).

(C)

The past	The present	The future

In consequence of their implicitly Euclidean conception of space, for the Atomists the infinitude of space coincided with its limitlessness. Lucretius formulates the theory in the words: "Wherever one may find himself, the universe stretches away from him uniformly and in every direction without bounds."[19] Lucretius gives reasons for this idea which may derive from the first Atomists. One of his reasons is: What is bounded, is always bounded by something else, outside it, and hence, since there is nothing outside the universe, it cannot be bounded. Another reason is this: Assume that the universe has a boundary and that someone who finds himself in the neighbourhood of this boundary shoots an arrow toward it. Either the arrow must continue through and past the boundary, or else it must be stopped there, by something that blocks its progress. Lucretius finds both alternatives unreasonable and thus concludes that the universe has no limit.

The Atomists believed that the infinite space contains an infinite number of worlds, each world being born to flourish for a time and then to disintegrate.

K. *The Euclidean and passive nature of space*

From the writings of the Atomists we gather that they held space to be infinite and uniform. There is no reason to suppose

[19] Ibid. I 966–7.

that they did not conceive of space in essentially the same way as Euclid and all the Greek mathematicians who contributed to the development of Euclidean geometry. Democritus was himself a mathematician who made significant contributions to geometry. (He is supposed to have anticipated the type of infinitesimal considerations Archimedes was later to develop with such mastery.)

The Atomists exhibited a very strong propensity to think that the motion of an atom is exclusively determined by its relation to other atoms, not by any properties of space itself. In the normal course of events, on their view, the way an atom moves depends entirely on how other atoms act upon it, through pressure and impact. To this extent, space is mechanically passive according to atomistic theory. The Epicurean assumption of an original fall of the atoms and/or an inherent tendency of the atoms to fall, with its implication of an absolute up–down direction in space, is, however, a lapse from the basic view.

L. *The fundamental role of mechanical concepts*

The early Atomists thought they could completely describe the atoms in terms of the concept of "fullness", "hardness" (materiality), and the concepts of space and time (shape, size, position, rest, and motion). Atoms, they claimed, do not have colour, odour, taste, or acoustical qualities; they have only fullness, size, shape, position, motion, or rest. The Epicureans added weight as an independent quality to this list. These notions can all be considered as mechanical concepts. The theory that atoms have no colour, odour, taste, etc., was to play a very great role in European philosophy from the seventeenth century on, when it was restated in the form that secondary sense qualities do not exist in the external world. The theory has the equally interesting consequence that only mechanical concepts need be considered in fundamental physical theory. The conceptual apparatus of Galilean-Newtonian mechanics is far more subtle and precise than that of Greek atomism. At the same time, however, this mechanics can be regarded as a magnificent, if only partial and temporary, verification of the consequence just mentioned.

M. *Determinism*

"Determinism" is a vague and ambiguous term. Keeping this reservation in mind, we may designate Leucippus' and Democritus' theory as the first great attempt to work out a consistently deterministic world view. The motions of the atoms take place by "necessity", in accordance with the laws of mechanics; there is no "chance" in the universe. Here, as on several other points, the Epicureans modified the original doctrine by their teaching that the atoms have the capacity to swerve, spontaneously and unpredictably, from their given paths.

The ancient atomic theory is, as already mentioned, in many respects an anticipation of Galilean-Newtonian mechanics, elaborated 2,000 years later, and of the accompanying mechanistic philosophy of nature.[20]

Not until the present century has physics definitely parted ways with the ancient Atomists. The particle structure of matter, the constancy of matter, absolute space, the homogeneity and passivity of space, as well as determinism, are all postulates which have now been modified or discarded.

The Atomists thought that with their means they could explain mental as well as material phenomena. They were thus the first radical materialists, if by a "materialist" is meant a person who maintains that "nothing but matter exists". The Atomists expressed their materialism thus:

> Only atoms and the void exist.

A corollary of this proposition is:

---

[20] As this is not a history of physics, I have intentionally not discussed in detail the laws of mechanics that the ancient Atomists postulated. It might be worth mentioning, however, that here also they were surprisingly modern on many points. The law of inertia, first formulated by Descartes, is stated by Newton as follows: "Every body continues in its state of rest or motion in a right line unless it is compelled to change that state by forces impressed upon it." Within his conceptual framework, Democritus came quite close to one part of this law when he asserted that atoms "by nature are at rest and are set in motion only through impact". (Diels, *Fragmente* 68 A 47.) Epicurus approximated the other part with his theory that an atom continues its motion through empty space until it is obstructed by other atoms. Galileo's discovery that the velocity of a freely falling body is independent of its weight was anticipated by the Epicurean theory that all atoms when falling freely through space move with the same velocity.

The soul consists of atoms (especially fine, smooth, and agile ones), and all mental processes are motions of atoms.

The Atomists thought that they could explain a wide range of psychic phenomena through their theory of images. All things continually left off thin surface films, each constituting a kind of image of the emitting thing. Perception consists of such an image permeating the pores of the sense organs. At times these images go astray or are altered during transfer or are formed in space without having any substantial archetypes. Thus is it possible to account for dreams and hallucinations and even for the appearance of gods.

A very general consequence of the basic assumptions of atomism is that material reality is essentially different from its appearance to our senses. We gain knowledge of the real constitution of things only by using reason to process and interpret the evidence of the senses. Democritus saw in this fact an epistemological problem which he wittily stated in a dialogue between Reason and the Senses. Reason says to the Senses: "Colour exists merely in the popular belief, and similarly with bitter and sweet; in reality only the void and atoms exist." The Senses reply: "Poor Reason, you have obtained your certainties from us, and now you wish to repudiate us by means of them? Our downfall will be your defeat."[21] At times considerations of this kind made Democritus doubt that we can reach genuine knowledge of the nature of things at all: ". . . we have no real knowledge of anything, but each one's opinion depends on the influx of perceptual images".[22] "We know, in fact, nothing, because truth is hidden in the depths."[23] In the analogous situation that obtained when the mechanistic philosophy of nature had been revived in the seventeenth century, the British empiricists, Locke, Berkeley, and Hume found themselves confronted with the same epistemological problem. The problem, which Democritus was the first to see, has played a central role in modern philosophical thought.

[21] Diels, *Die Fragmente der Vorsokratiker*, 68 B 125.
[22] Ibid. 68 B 7.
[23] Ibid. 68 B 117.

7. THE LATER FATE OF NATURAL PHILOSOPHY

The tradition of natural philosophy which Thales initiated at the beginning of the sixth century BC did not come to an end with Democritus' atomism. After attaining its culmination with the Atomists, however, it survived mainly as a subordinate part of philosophical systems that satisfied needs quite different from the early natural philosophers' desire to see how the machinery of the universe functioned.

The atomistic world without God, divine purpose, or immortal souls must have been something truly detestable for the religious Plato. A telling fact is that whereas he discussed so many earlier philosophers by name, he never refers to Democritus. Aristotle presents atomistic ideas quite thoroughly, but only in order to refute them. The Epicureans, who adopted and modified the atomic theory, valued it for the very reasons that must have made Plato detest it.

Socrates did not approve of the interests of the natural philosophers, in part because he disliked the causal explanations they arrived at, and in part also because he considered the study of nature a misuse of the time man is granted, which he could use better for moral reflection and self-improvement. Plato followed him in this and gave his own dislike a metaphysical justification through the theory that the world of the senses is a pseudo-reality about which only half-truths can be stated.

A. *Plato's* Timaeus

In the *Timaeus* Plato sets forth a natural philosophy which he did not himself take as a literal truth but which has had an enormous historical influence. On first inspection, and to anyone who has never travelled any large distance, the world looks as if it were a hemisphere with the surface of the earth as its floor and the sky as its vault. Thales' world picture had much in common with this initial impression. For those who have travelled more, this first impression gives way to the impression that the world is a sphere with the earth resting in its centre. The Atomists, with their infinite universe, had gone far beyond this second impression, but Plato returned to it. Despite his contempt for the evidence of the senses, he kept much closer on this point to the crude sense impressions than his predecessors had done. The motive was surely religious: to uphold the dignity of man and God and the importance of the earth, man's home, in the universe.

Plato's theory of matter in the *Timaeus* is a synthesis of ideas which he borrowed from Empedocles, the Pythagoreans, and the Atomists. From Empedocles he took the idea of the four elements: earth, air, fire, and water. The Atomists' notion of atoms inspired him to assume that each element occurs in the form of elementary particles with characteristics specific to that element. From the Pythagoreans he borrowed the idea that reality can be described in mathematical terms. All the elementary particles of a given element have a common geometrical shape, and these shapes are all those of regular polyhedra. (The elementary particles of earth are cubes, those of water icosahedra, those of air octahedra, and those of fire tetrahedra.) Unlike the Atomists, he does not impute absolute indivisibility to his elementary particles. One particle can be split up into several particles, and several can merge into one. In contrast to Empedocles he does not ascribe immutability to the elements, with the exception of earth. By mathematical operations upon the triangles into which the sides of a polyhedron can be decomposed, water, air, and fire may be transformed into one another.

The basis of these geometrically characterized elementary particles is space itself, which Plato describes in words reminiscent of how the earlier natural philosophers described their primary substances. It is eternal, in itself without any form, but able to assume all forms.

Contrary to his predecessors, Plato gave large scope to teleological explanations and anthropomorphic and theological ideas in his natural philosophy (§ 17). On this score, as on so many others, he took a step backward relative to the positions already reached.

B. *Aristotle*

Aristotle's ideas are substantially a modification of Plato's. Aristotle's universe, like Plato's, is a finite sphere with the earth in the centre. The role of space in the *Timaeus* is taken over by "first matter" in Aristotle's philosophy; in itself it has no definite forms or characteristics but it can take on any form, any characteristic. To Empedocles' and Plato's four elements Aristotle added a fifth, the celestial aether, which fills up space beyond the orbit of the moon. Aristotle had no sympathy for Plato's mathematical fantasies, but his theory of the elements is otherwise closely related to Plato's. The part that triangles and polyhedra play for Plato is assumed in Aristotle by the classical opposites: wet–dry, cold–warm. The earth is characterized by coldness and dryness, water by coldness and moisture, air by moisture and heat, and fire by heat and dryness. By substitutions of one quality for its opposite, each of the four elements can change into any other. This part of Aristotle's theory can be illustrated, as in diagram (D). Unlike the Atomists and Plato, however, Aristotle did not postulate elementary particles.

(D)

Like Plato, Aristotle made extensive use of teleological explanations and theological hypotheses in his natural philosophy (§§22–3).

Even if Aristotle made some attempts, especially in his mechanics, to present his theories in a mathematical form, there is in this respect an obvious difference between Plato's and Aristotle's modes of thought in natural philosophy. While Plato's thought frequently moves in geometrical orbits, Aristotle generally thinks in qualitative terms. This difference is of interest because of its later reflection in the development of ideas during late medieval times and the Renaissance. Many thinkers of the fourteenth century, it is true, paid special attention to, and further developed, the mathematical aspects of Aristotle's natural philosophy (§59). However, the renewed study of Plato that the Renaissance brought about was a great source of inspiration for the mathematical approach, characteristic of the new natural science. Kepler, for example, was inspired, and sometimes led astray, by Platonic views when, with infinite pains, he deciphered his planetary laws from Tycho Brahe's observations. Newton inherited several of his ideas from the seventeenth-century Cambridge Platonists.

C. *Plato's scepticism in natural philosophy*

Plato's thoughts on natural philosophy are, contrary to Aristotle's, marked by a deep scepticism concerning our ability to reach genuine knowledge in this domain. His scepticism had several roots. One was metaphysical: the world of the senses does not possess full reality; the only true reality is the world of Ideas; now the validity of knowledge is directly proportional to the degree of reality of its object; hence, we can form no more than "opinions" about the world of the senses. Another cause for his scepticism was the insight that the mathematical descriptions of phenomena are never more than approximately correct: nothing moves in exactly that circle, or spiral, or what not, that mathematical physics ascribes to it. A third cause for Plato's scepticism was probably his awareness of the theoretical distance between observed phenomena and the geometrical theory which, according to his famous words, serves to "save them" (§16 E). Although Plato did not work out his view in detail, perhaps it is not too daring to attribute to him a consciousness of the fact that phenomena can, in principle, be saved in several ways, through several distinct geometrical theories. The sceptical Plato presented his own cosmology in the *Timaeus* merely as a likely story.

Seen as a reaction against the *naïveté* of many previous philosophers, Plato's scepticism may appear healthy, but unfortunately it was combined with a strongly negative evaluation of nature and empirical research (§16 D).

D. *Stoics and Epicureans*

The Stoics and the Epicureans were the only post-Aristotelian schools of philosophy that genuinely carried on the tradition of natural philosophy. Neither of them, however, retained the Milesians' youthful curiosity about the world. Both schools often chose their positions on problems of natural philosophy with a view to the mental peace of man. The Stoics adopted many of their ideas from Heraclitus whose interest in natural philosophy already resembled the interest of a religious prophet in his theology.

As Sambursky has shown, under its theologico-moral colouring, Stoic physics contains a number of interesting thoughts on the notions of continuity and force. According to Sambursky's fascinating judgement, the Stoic and Epicurean doctrines appear as archetypal contrasts. Whereas the Epicureans made exclusive use of the particle concept and a primitively mechanistic explanatory model, Stoic physics was founded on the idea of a matter spread continuously in space and subject to a dynamic play of forces. Whereas the world of the Epicureans resembled a mechanical machine, the world of the Stoics, like that of Plato, was analogous to a biological organism.

Generally speaking, Plato initiated a schism between empirical research and speculative philosophy which, in spite of many exceptions, came to stay. The most remarkable contributions of post-Democritean ancient philosophy fall within domains other than those that occupied the interest of the natural philosophers.

II

Religion and Mathematics

8. A PHILOSOPHICAL COMPLEX

The outlook of early Greek natural philosophy was essentially monistic. No sharp boundaries were drawn between different regions of reality, from the point of view of knowledge or of feeling or of evaluation. This monism already appears in the fundamental idea that everything there is can be reduced to a single primary substance. In the Pythagoreans, the Eleatics, and Plato, the philosophers we shall consider in this chapter, we find an intensive dualism. For them reality falls apart into several regions which differ profoundly, in reality, in value, and in accessibility to knowledge.

The Pythagoreans made lists of "opposites", which they considered essential to the understanding of the world. Such a list is recorded by Aristotle (list I).[1]

(I)			
	Limit	— Unlimited	(1)
	Odd	— Even	(2)
	Unity	— Multiplicity	(3)
	Right	— Left	(4)
	Male	— Female	(5)
	Rest	— Motion	(6)
	Straight	— Crooked	(7)
	Light	— Darkness	(8)
	Good	— Evil	(9)
	Square	— Rectangle	(10)

It is tempting to dismiss this as sheer abracadabra, but that would be a mistake. Although the list is not the expression of any deep wisdom, it is a key to the understanding of a powerful current, at once intellectual and emotional, in the history of philosophy. We shall come quite near its source in this chapter. Let us look more closely at the opposites listed. Five of the pairs, (1), (2), (3), (7), and (10),

[1] Aristotle, *Metaphysics*, I 5, 986ᵃ 22 ff.

are bound up with the mathematics of the Pythagoreans and their mathematically saturated physics and metaphysics. It would lead us too far astray to try to disentangle the complex speculation these five pairs stem from. Pair (4) appears to be an unadapted remnant of the primitive magico-religious ideas that lie at the base of this entire mode of thinking. It should be noted that the pairs are somehow parallel. The left-hand column as a whole stands in opposition to the right-hand column as a whole, and within each column the terms lend each other colour, so to speak. Through the pairs (3), (6), (8), and (9), unity, rest, light, and goodness are thus together contrasted with multiplicity, motion, darkness, and evil. Pair (5) gives us the outlook on woman, characteristic of male society and of the philosophic ascetic. She, the inferior and the object of man's sexual desire, belongs to the worse half of reality.

The Eleatic school founded by Parmenides also held a dualistic view of the world. Parmenides contrasts the way of truth, leading to knowledge of what is truly real, and the way of illusion, ensnaring us in what the senses hold out. If we combine some of the properties characteristic of true reality and the opposite properties which the illusory world exhibits, we obtain the pairs of opposites in list II'.

(II')	Unity	—	Multiplicity
	Rest	—	Motion
	Unchangeableness	—	Change
	Eternity	—	Creation and Destruction
	Reality	—	Unreality (a)

To this list we may add another (II″) which concerns our comprehension of the two realities:

(II″)	Reason	—	The Senses
	Truth	—	Falsehood
	Certainty	—	Uncertainty

The antithesis (a) is carried by Parmenides to such an extreme that his dualism almost cancels itself out; the illusory reality characterized by the concepts in the right-hand column simply does not exist.

Plato's dualism harbours almost all the ingredients found

in his predecessors plus a few more. The central antithesis
in Plato's philosophy around which all the others are grouped
is the one of which, presumably, he was the author:

(III′)   Ideas — Sensible Objects

Ideas have the nature of a limit. They are principles which
unify a multiplicity of sensible objects. They are to the world
of the senses as man is to woman. They exist in repose and
light and, at least according to one of Plato's thoughts, they
constitute what is truly good. The truth which we discover
with the help of reason is concerned with them. The objects
of the senses are in all these respects of a contrary nature.
In Plato's thought certain pairs of opposites (III″) were
closely connected with (III′):

(III″)   Dialectics (logic)
          and Mathematics   — Empirical Science
          Certainty   — Likelihood

and above all:

(III‴)   Soul — Body

The dualism is not the same in the Pythagoreans, the
Eleatics, and Plato, but the sets of antitheses that occupied
them overlap. The situation can be illustrated, as in diagram
(E).

(E)

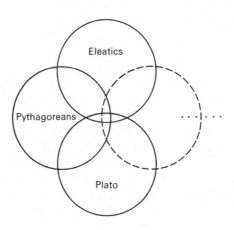

The dualism I am now talking of is not *one* theory, nor is it more than in part *theory*. It is rather a psychological complex, or a historic chain of psychological complexes intimately linked to each other. By the word "complex" I mean a relatively stable combination of emotions and ideas the occurrence of which in a particular thinker is largely due to irrational motives. When I call this dualism a complex, I do not imply that all the ideas that are involved are erroneous, or that the emotions are all distorted or unjustified. Correct or fruitful ideas and sound and noble feelings may of course form parts of a complex.

The Platonic complex reappears in milder form in Aristotle. He struggles against it, it does not really suit him, and yet he never succeeds in freeing himself from its grip. During the closing centuries of antiquity, the complex flared up to an intensified life among the neo-Pythagoreans and neo-Platonists. From neo-Platonism it was inherited by the philosophy of Christianity, with St. Augustine as one of the most important interpreters. In Christianity the complex regained contact with the kind of popular religious belief from which it had originally sprouted. It acquired new elements and came to dominate medieval philosophy in Europe. It recurs also in many of the great classic philosophers of modern times.

The title of this chapter, Religion and Mathematics, indicates two of the chief factors that seem to have nourished the complex among Greek philosophers.

Greek religion, like most religions, contained many different layers deposited throughout the ages. In part it was a belief in divine forces of various kinds, a belief demanding rites and sacrifices but not much more besides. In part it was also a belief in a moral order which makes punishment follow upon crime and in which the divine powers are fitted as instruments of justice. With the so-called mysteries, however, especially those of the Orphic variety, another kind of religiousness appeared at the beginning of the sixth century. Only the initiated (*mystes*) was permitted to participate in the mystic rites, which were believed to effect salvation from the troubles of life and guarantee a happier existence beyond the grave. The idea of the soul as man's better and imperishable part played an important role, *"soma sema"* (the body a tomb) was a mystic saying. The mysteries often had the character of a divine drama in which the members took part, thus joining in the life of the gods. To "see" the Holy for oneself was the goal of the *mystes*, and the most advanced initiates were also called "seers". It appears that our dualistic philosophers took many of their ideas from the Orphic mysteries. They were prone to conceive of their own role as philosophers according to the following equations:

The philosopher	=	The mystical initiated
The non-philosopher	=	The uninitiated

The worship of the stars, which may well have been an original element of Greek religion (possibly stimulated by contact with the Orient), was the source of another aspect of Plato's dualism:

(III'''')   The heavenly bodies   ——   The Earth

From Plato this idea passed over to Aristotle, and from him to the medieval scholastics, and even as late as the sixteenth and seventeenth centuries it still offered stubborn resistance to the new physics and astronomy.

Another factor that influenced the dualistic philosophers was mathematics. The history of early Greek mathematics was indeed tightly interwoven with the development of dualistic philosophy. The Pythagoreans are supposed to have been the first to develop mathematics as an abstract deductive science, and the Platonic Academy was a mathematical centre in Athens during the fourth century. Plato believed that mathematics dealt with a realm of intelligible objects akin to the ideas, and the superior certainty the method of mathematics seemed to provide inspired him with the desire to emulate this method in philosophy. Parmenides and his pupils had already tried to prove their theories in a deductive manner.

The dualism which so systematically ranks things as higher and lower can naturally develop into, or become associated with, ideas of more complex ranking orders. In Plato's philosophy one encounters many such ideas. Some of the orders of rank that he considered are:

God—men—women—animals
Philosophers—warriors—labourers
Dialectics—mathematics—natural science

The idea of strict orders of rank is in Plato not only an element of philosophical theory but also a part of a political ideal. In the neo-Platonists and in many other later representatives of dualism, the hierarchical mode of thinking is even more elaborate and systematic.

9. EVERYTHING IS NUMBER: THE PYTHAGOREANS

Pythagoras (born in Asia Minor) was active in southern Italy, probably about the middle of the sixth century. He organized a sect whose varied interests included not only scientific investigation but also political activity and a religion of the mystic type. For some time the sect had great power in southern Italy and Sicily, but it then met resistance and was crushed about the middle of the fifth century. The best-known member of the sect was the philosopher and physician Alcmaeon (*c*.500 BC). In the fourth century BC Pythagoreanism was revived in southern Italy by Philolaus of Crotona and Archytas of Tarentum, a personal friend of Plato's. Within this new Pythagorean school certain non-geocentric astronomical theories were developed, which in turn led Aristarchus of Samos (beginning of the third century BC), the Copernicus of antiquity, to propound a heliocentric theory. Even after Pythagoreanism had disappeared as a philosophico-scientific school, it survived in the form of a mystical religious movement. The hectic flowering of mystic religions during the first centuries AD brought a final upsurge to this sect as well.

The Pythagoreans made significant contributions to the development of Greek mathematics in number theory as well as in geometry. They were interested not only in what we would now call pure mathematics but also in the application of mathematics to physical phenomena. It seems to have been their discoveries in acoustics that led them to the opinion that all scientific knowledge can be formulated mathematically. Aristotle writes:

They also perceived the relations and laws of musical harmony in number, and then everything in its entire nature seemed formed from number as its prototype, which is in turn the first in all nature, so that they [the Pythagoreans] assumed that the elements of number are the elements of everything and that the entire world is harmony and number.[2]

The only numbers the Pythagoreans knew of were the positive integers: 1, 2, 3 . . . Their mathematical philosophy of nature implied that the essence of reality can be expressed by means of these integers.

The so-called Pythagorean Theorem asserts that the square (*A*) on the hypotenuse (*a*) of a right-angled triangle is equal in area to the sum of the squares (*B* and *C*) on the other two sides (*b* and *c*):

(i) $A = B + C$

(F)

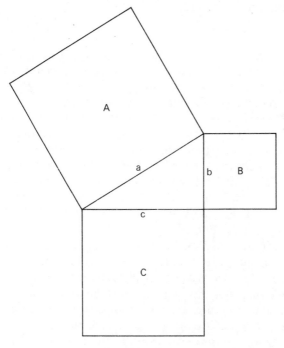

[2] Ibid., I 5, 985[b] 32 ff.

Special cases of this theorem were already familiar to the Babylonian mathematicians several thousand years BC, but the discovery of the general law and its proof seems to be due to the Pythagorean school. In connection with this theorem the Pythagoreans made a remarkable mathematical discovery. Let us suppose that the legs of the right-angled triangle have the same length: $b = c$. How long, then, is the hypotenuse? If everything can be described with the help of the positive integers, it should be possible to find some unit of measure such that the legs as well as the hypotenuse are integral multiples of it. Assume that m is such a unit and that $a = x \cdot m$ and $b = c = y \cdot m$, where x and y are two of the integers: 1, 2, 3 . . . If the square on m is M, we get: $A = x^2 \cdot M$, and $B = C = y^2 \cdot M$. According to the Pythagorean theorem (i) it should then be the case that:

(ii) $x^2 \cdot M = y^2 \cdot M + y^2 \cdot M,$

and hence that the purely arithmetical equation:

(iii) $x^2 = 2y^2$

holds for two numbers x and y from the sequence 1, 2, 3 . . . The Pythagoreans found a proof, of a very elementary kind, showing that such is not the case. When the legs of a right-angled triangle are of the same length there is thus no common unit of measure of which the legs and the hypotenuse are integral multiples: the hypotenuse is "incommensurable" (does not have a common unit of measure) with the legs. The Pythagoreans are said to have considered this discovery to be such a theoretical scandal that they tried to keep it a secret among the members of the sect. It was in stark conflict with their philosophical creed that "the entire world is harmony and number".

The Milesian idea of a natural explanation of whatever happens in the world was complemented by the Pythagoreans with the idea of a mathematical formulation of the explanation. Among the Pythagoreans themselves, however, this fruitful idea did not lead to significant scientific progress outside pure mathematics and harmonics. In theories belonging to natural philosophy, they seem to have been guided by a mathematical speculation which did not take sufficient account of experience. Certain numerical relationships were assumed to be more perfect than others, and they wished to see the more perfect realized in nature.

Their scientific interests fused with their religious ideas. They believed in the transmigration of souls and in the power of asceticism to deliver the souls from such transmigration. They set up a strange system of ritual prescriptions for the conduct of daily life, and they seem to have conceived of mathematical speculation as communion with a divine reality.

10. BEING AND NON-BEING: THE ELEATICS

Parmenides, who lived in southern Italy during the first half of the fifth century, manifests in an extreme form the faith in the power of abstract logical thought that is found among the Pythagoreans. As logical axioms he stated the propositions: "Being (or: what is) is", and "Non-being (or: what is not, or: nothing) is not."[3] By abstruse arguments, the details of which may be omitted here, he deduced his philosophy from these axioms. Briefly summarized, it asserts that being is a single, homogeneous, indivisible, unchangeable, unmovable, timeless, spherical body and that it is identical with thought. The senses present illusions only.

The course of human thought is incalculable. It is an interesting fact that Parmenides' metaphysics was reportedly one of the foremost sources of inspiration for the Atomists (as well as for Empedocles and Anaxagoras), and that this metaphysics thus belongs to the intellectual background of the mechanistic world view. The Atomists, Aristotle says, broke up Parmenides' unique, unchangeable reality into a multitude of small intrinsically unchangeable particles, the atoms, in order to be able to account for the world of the senses.

Parmenides' paradoxical theory gained an astute apologist in his pupil Zeno of Elea. Parmenides' theory includes the two propositions:

A. Plurality does not exist
B. Motion does not exist

---

[3] Diels, *Die Fragmente der Vorsokratiker*, 28 B 2, 6, 7.

These propositions, which patently contradict all our observations, must have exposed Parmenides to derisive attacks. Diogenes of Sinope refuted proposition B by walking, just as Dr Johnson was later to refute Berkeley's immaterialism by kicking a stone. Zeno wanted to repay Parmenides' assailants in the same coin by showing that their views led to ludicrous consequences. Thus, Zeno wished to demonstrate that each of the two assumptions:

A'. Plurality exists
B'. Motion exists

leads to absurd conclusions. His arguments, known as Zeno's Paradoxes, are perhaps more interesting than the theory they were intended to defend.

Three of these arguments were:

1. (Against plurality): All plurality is a plurality of units. But no object to be found in reality is a unit. Since there are not units, neither is there any plurality.

2. "Achilles and the Tortoise" against motion; (see (G)). Achilles, A, the fleetest of men, runs a race with a tortoise, T, the slowest of quadrupeds. At the start of the race, A is at point a_0, and T, who has a head-start, is at point a_1. In order to overtake T, A must first reach the point a_1, but by then T has already gone on to point a_2. When A reaches a_2, T has attained the point a_3, and so on indefinitely. Thus A can never catch up with T.

(G)

a_0		a_1	a_2	a_3	

3. "The Arrow" against motion: When an arrow flies through the air, it must at every instant be in a certain place (Aristotle: "occupy a space equal to itself").[4] But if the arrow *is* in a certain place at a certain instant, then at that instant it is at rest. At every instant, therefore, the arrow is at rest.

These paradoxes of Zeno's have given rise to a debate which is still going on.

Plato seems to have indicated a satisfactory solution to the first of these paradoxes. He notes that the question of

[4] Aristotle, *Physics*, VI 9, 239^b 6.

"one or many" is relative to the point of view from which it is asked. Let us suppose that we are standing in front of seven persons, and someone asks us to count. Before we can comply with this request, we must have a unit of reckoning. If the unit is the concept "person", then we may say of each one of the seven that he is one (person), and we may assert that there are seven (persons). But if the unit is the concept "rib", then each of the seven represents many ribs. What from one viewpoint (with reference to one unit of reckoning) is one, may thus from another viewpoint (with reference to another unit of reckoning) be many. On the basis of this distinction, Plato rejects the first paradox as a sophism—which does not prevent him, however, from falling victim at times to sophistic arguments of a very similar kind.[5]

The second paradox is apparently based on a confusion between two propositions which are widely different in meaning, viz:

(i) There exist infinitely many instants, after the start of the race, at which T still has the lead over A.

(ii) There exists no instant, after the start, at which T no longer has the lead over A.

Zeno proved proposition (i) even though he did not explicitly state the premisses for his proof, and it thus has a rather indefinite intuitive character. From (i), however, (ii) does not follow. Nevertheless, it must be (ii) that Zeno really wished to prove. If his conclusion does not amount to (ii), there is hardly any reason for speaking of a paradox.

The difference between (i) and (ii) can be clarified effectively through a well-known elementary mathematical consideration. Let us choose our unit of length so that the interval $a_0\text{-}a_1$ has unit length. Let us further assume that A runs with constant speed and let us mark our dial so that A moves a unit of length per each unit of time. We also assume the speed of T to be constant but less than A's, say (generously) $\frac{1}{2}$. Let t_i be the time it takes A to get from point a_{i-1} to a_i. We then see:

[5] Plato, *Parmenides*, 129 c–d. Cf. Plato, *Republic*, 524 d–525 a and *Parmenides*, 165 e.

$$t_1 = 1 \quad t_2 = \tfrac{1}{2} \quad t_3 = \tfrac{1}{4} \text{ etc.}$$

and in general:

$$t_i = \frac{1}{2^{i-1}}$$

Concerning the sum $\Sigma_n = t_1 + t_2 + \ldots + t_n$ it is easily found:

$$\Sigma_n = 2 - \frac{1}{2^{n-1}}$$

When n increases Σ_n increases and can be made to approach 2 as close as we like without ever becoming 2. This means that A passes T exactly 2 units of time after the start.

One may also ask how matters really stand with Zeno's intuitive proof of (i). The unstated premisses for this proof must include the assumption of some kind of continuity of motion (the word "continuity" here not taken in its strict mathematical sense). But of course it cannot be proved *a priori* that the motion of bodies is continuous. With good reason it can also be doubted whether it is possible either to prove to to disprove it in an empirical manner. "Cinematographic" motion, in which the jumps are so minute that they defy observation, would for us be indistinguishable from continuous motion. Perhaps the premisses of Zeno's proof of (i) thus include an unrealistic assumption. The idea that motion is cinematographic was, I think, first proposed in medieval Arabic-Jewish philosophy. In our own time it has been revived, in a discussion of Zeno's paradoxes, by the mathematicians David Hilbert and Paul Bernays.

The third paradox is based on two separate assumptions:

(i) If the body B is in motion at instant t, then B is in some position p at t.

(ii) If B is in a position p at t, then B is not moving at t.

From (i) and (ii) it follows directly that:

(iii) If B is in motion at t, then B is not in motion at t.

Since B and t may be chosen arbitrarily, (iii) implies:

(iv) No body is in motion at any time,

which is the Parmenidean assertion.

Let us look more closely at the premises of this inference. What is meant in them by the statement that B is in motion at t? Since Zeno has been dead now for more than 2,000 years, it is better to change the question to: What might reasonably be meant by this statement? If we suppose, as modern physics does, that a body B *is* in a position p at time t, whether or not B is then at rest or in motion, the difference between rest and motion at t must be defined in terms of B's positions at the moments surrounding t. One might, e.g., say that B is at rest at t, if there is some interval of time enclosing t during which B uninterruptedly occupies the same position as at t. More sophisticated notions of rest and motion are also possible. (We can, e.g., introduce the position function $p(t) = $ 'B's position at t' and assume, with physics, that time is a linear continuum, that $p(t)$ is defined for each instant t within some interval of this continuum, and finally also that $p(t)$ is a continuous and differentiable function. If all these assumptions are made—their literal "truth" is, of course, debatable— the statement that B rests at t_0 can be construed as meaning that B's momentary speed at t_0, i.e. the first derivative of $p(t)$ for $t = t_0$, is zero.) If we understand the premises of Paradox 3 in accordance with some such definition, it is seen that premiss (ii) is an unjustified assertion. Aristotle criticized Paradox 3 in several ways: one of his objections resembles the present critique—although he declines to speak of a body as being at rest or moving in a certain instant.[6]

Zeno's paradoxes all have an essentially mathematical character. In Paradox 2 we can discern a sort of intellectual uneasiness with the infinite and this recurs in other paradoxes ascribed to Zeno. In one of his arguments against plurality, he states that if there is a plurality of things, it must be both finite and infinite. We may disregard here how he tried to prove that plurality must be infinite. That it must be finite follows, he thinks, from the fact that "things must be just as many as they are, and neither more nor less".[7] Zeno thus contends that:

---

[6] Aristotle, *Physics*, VI 8, 239^a 27 ff.
[7] Diels, *Die Fragmente der Vorsokratiker*, 29 B 3.

(i) If a set S is equal in number of elements to S, then S is finite.

From this we get by contraposition:

(ii) If a set S is infinite, then S is not equal in number of elements to S.

From (ii) we can, of course, safely conclude:

(iii) No infinite set exists.

In this paradox Zeno apparently maintains that the concept of an 'infinite set' contains a contradiction. He may therefore be regarded as the first representative of the finitary approach, which was given its classic formulation in antiquity by Aristotle.

How could Zeno assert (i), and therewith implicitly (ii) and (iii)? Perhaps he had an intimation of a classic paradox which turns up several times in late antiquity (e.g. in the commentary on Euclid by the neo-Platonic, Proclos) and was noticed in more recent times by men such as Galileo, Leibniz, and Bolzano, until it was transformed by Cantor into a legitimate theorem of set theory. If we assume the existence of the infinite sequence of numbers $N = \{1, 2, 3 \ldots\}$, then we may consider the correspondence (H).

(H)

$$
\begin{array}{ccccccc}
1 & 2 & 3 & 4 & \cdots & n & \cdots \\
\updownarrow & \updownarrow & \updownarrow & \updownarrow & & \updownarrow & \\
1 \quad\quad 2 & 3 & 4 & 5 & 6 & \cdots & n+2 \quad \cdots
\end{array}
$$

Is it not obvious here that N is equal in number of elements to $N' = \{3, 4, 5 \ldots\}$? But N is $\{1, 2\} + N'$. Does this not show that N' is less than N in number of elements? It seems, thus, that N is equal to N', which is less than N, and, hence, that N is less than N, in number of elements. Such an argument may possibly lie behind Zeno's assumption (i). The error consists in our mis-stating what we actually see. What we see is that the set N can be put into one-to-one correspondence with one of its proper subsets, N'. But in order to be able to speak of the number of elements in these sets we must first define the concept 'number of elements' in an adequate manner for infinite sets. Two thousand years after Zeno's lifetime such a definition was given by Cantor who thus made possible a correct description of what we see.

11. SOCRATES AND PLATO

At the age of about twenty the Athenian Plato (427–347 BC) came in contact with the street character, the genius and martyr, Socrates, who spent his time in discussions with the citizens of Athens. Socrates was especially interested in moral problems. What is good? What is virtue? What is right and what is wrong? He believed that the surest way of settling such questions was to define the meaning of the terms involved, i.e. such words as "good", "virtue", "right", "wrong". In the year 399 BC, after standing trial for impiety, he was sentenced to death and drank the cup of hemlock. By his moral stature, his insistence on conceptual clarity, and his tragic death, Socrates made an indelible impression on Plato. Plato's writings are all in the form of dialogue, and in most of them Socrates is the major speaker and apparently Plato's own spokesman. Unfortunately, we have no effective method of deciding which of the views that Socrates is made to pronounce were actually his, and which Plato alone is responsible for. The dialogues are outstanding documents in the history of thought, and many of them, such as the *Apology*, the *Symposium* and the *Phaedo*, are masterpieces of world literature. Besides philosophy and science (especially mathematics) Plato's interests included politics. His ideal state, which he described in his two longest works, the *Republic* and the *Laws*, was a hierarchical, strictly regulated society governed by an élite of philosophers and with such characteristics of a totalitarian state as censorship, organized propaganda, and manipulative eugenic policy. His repeated attempts to put his theories into actual practice in Sicily failed ignominiously. In Athens he founded a school, the Academy, which was to last until AD 529, when the Christian emperor Justinian dissolved it and confiscated its property. In addition to philosophy, the mathematical sciences were cultivated at the Academy, and many of the foremost mathematicians of the fourth century belonged to it or were under its influence. The Alexandrian mathematician, Euclid, who wrote the textbook in geometry that was to become standard for 2,000 years, probably received his education at the Academy.

Socrates' interest in the investigation of concepts and definitions was no doubt something new in Greek philosophy. Naturally, earlier philosophers must have clarified the meaning of one term or another. Nor can Socrates have been the first Greek to set up definitions; in mathematics, astronomy, and medicine they must have appeared very early. The novelty of Socrates' approach was his concentration upon definitions and his epistemological expectations in connection with them. Since he has not left any writings, Plato became the first to introduce this interest in definitions into philosophical literature. It reappears in the works of Aristotle, whose analyses of concepts are much more subtle than those of Socrates and Plato. From the times of Plato and Aristotle it runs like a leitmotiv through the entire history of philosophy. Conceptual analysis as met with in Socrates, Plato, and Aristotle, will be taken up separately in Chapter IV.

Of Plato's many contributions to philosophical discussion, I shall here consider especially his theory of Ideas (§§ 12–15) and his philosophy of science (§ 16). His important notion of the soul and his natural philosophy, which has already been touched upon in § 7, will also be discussed very briefly (§ 17).

12. THE THEORY OF IDEAS AS A LOGICAL THEORY

The theory of Ideas is closely related to the Socratic–Platonic analysis of concepts. While Socrates posed questions such as "What is virtue?", "What is right?", and expected general definitions in reply, in Plato this interest was gradually transferred to another type of question: "This virtue, this justice, and so on, which the general definitions concern, what kind of reality are they?" Plato's famous theory of Ideas was an attempt to answer this. His answer was in brief that they are eternal, intelligible realities, "Ideas" or "Forms", which we perceive by our reason and of which things of the sensible world "partake".

The theory of Ideas as presented in Plato's dialogues is a multi-faceted doctrine. In what follows, I shall permit myself to sort out its various constituents under four headings, viz. logical theory, semantic theory, psychology and epistemology, and metaphysics. Let us first consider the logical aspect.

What is expressed by the statement:

Socrates is a man

can also be expressed, according to Plato, by the following statements, which both say the same thing:

Socrates partakes of the Idea of Man
The Idea of Man is present in Socrates

Instead of the "Idea (*eidos, idea*) of Man", Plato often speaks of the "nature" (*physis*) common to all men, or the "genus" (*genos*) to which all humans, and only they, belong, or the "essence" (*ousia*) which is characteristic of a human being. What is true of the word "man" is true of all, or at least of very many, similar words which we predicate of several things: "horse", "ox", "couch", "table", "beautiful", "green", "blue", "large", "small", etc. According to Plato, the three statements: 'The couch is large', 'The couch partakes of the Idea of Largeness', 'The Idea of Largeness is present in the couch', thus all express the same fact.

Plato's dialogues are not scientific treatises, and one can search in vain for a systematic exposition of his views on one problem or another. Nor did Plato ever set forth his theory of Ideas in one body. As a way of thinking and reasoning, it is present, however, almost everywhere in his writings. Plato argues, more or less consistently, and more or less explicitly, in accordance with certain general principles which may be called the logical axioms of the theory of Ideas, and to which I shall now give an abstract formulation, which they never received in Plato.

Axiom schema I. Being X is the same as partaking of the Idea of X-ness.

In this schema we may substitute for 'X' any of the terms mentioned above, and we thus obtain the special axioms which the schema covers. For example: 'Being a man is the same as partaking of the Idea of Man'. From this axiom schema we can immediately infer the schematic corollary:

Corollary A: There exists some Idea I such that being X is the same as partaking of I.

Axiom schema II: If being X is the same as partaking of the Idea I and the same as partaking of the Idea I', then I is identical with I'.

When the same substitution is made here, we obtain the special axiom: 'If being a man is the same as partaking of I and the same as partaking of I', then I is identical with I'.' The corollary A and this second schema give rise to the new schematic corollary:

Corollary B: There exists exactly one Idea I such that being X is the same as partaking of I.

Thus, for example, there exists exactly one Idea such that being a man and partaking of this Idea coincide.

Axiom schema III. An Idea is distinct from anything that partakes of that Idea.

These axioms have an obvious relationship to certain theorems of logic and set-theory. Let us replace "Idea" by "set", "partakes" by "is an element", and the whole phrase "being X is the same as partaking of I" by "it holds for all a that a is X if and only if a is an element of I". This replacement turns corollary A into:

(i) There exists a set I such that it holds for all a that a is X if and only if a is an element of I.

The same replacement transforms axiom schema II into:

(ii) If it holds for all a that (a) a is X if and only if a is an element of I, and (b) a is X if and only if a is an element of I', then I is identical with I'.

Each instance of this schema (ii) is a special case of the more general proposition:

(iii) If it holds for all a that a is an element of I if and only if a is an element of I', then I is identical with I'.

Schemata of type (i) play an important role in modern set-theory under the name of axioms of comprehension. The proposition (iii) is the so-called axiom of extensionality of modern set-theory. The founder of set-theory, Georg Cantor, considered Plato as one of his earliest precursors.

However, it is by no means certain that the above replacement of Platonic expressions by set-theoretical ones gives a historically correct interpretation of Plato's theory. The two statements:

a is an element of the set *S*

a has the property *P*

are closely related. If *a* is an element of the set *S*, then *a* has the property of being such an element; and if *a* has the property *P*, then *a* belongs to the set of all those things which have *P*, provided that there is such a set. But sets and properties are nevertheless not the same. The concept of set is so constituted that sets are identical if they have precisely the same elements. On the other hand, two properties can very well belong to exactly the same entities without being identical. The property of 'being a professor of philosophy at Uppsala in 1972' is obviously different in meaning from the property of 'having written either *Belief and Knowledge* or *Provability in Logic*', but the first property belongs to exactly the same two persons as the second. Now, is Plato's concept of Idea closer to our concept of set than it is to our concept of property? As a matter of fact, Plato's statements on this question are very indefinite. Evidence can be adduced from his works for a set as well as for a property interpretation of the concept of Idea. The historical truth is probably that Plato was not clearly aware of our distinction between sets and properties. He might possibly have been inclined to assert that, although everything that is *X* is also *Y*, and conversely, there is a single Idea by which the *X*s are *X* and a distinct single Idea by which the same entities are *Y*.

Schemata I and II lack definite scope until it is specified which expressions may be substituted for the letter '*X*'. Nowhere in Plato's works is there to be found an unambiguous view on this point. He sometimes seems to permit substitution of any word or expression whatsoever that can be meaningfully predicated of several things. We may call this Plato's *tolerant view*. Sometimes, however, he seems inclined to permit only some such expressions as substituends. Exactly which expressions, however, he never succeeded in clearly indicating. Plato's attempt to formulate a, let us say, *restrictive view* is connected with what I have called the dualistic complex. Ideas belong to the better half of reality, and it is therefore repugnant to Plato to allow the substitution of words that represent base and unpleasant things like, say, the word "filth". In the dialogue *Parmenides*, which includes some shrewd self-criticism, Plato makes Parmenides the Eleatic reproach Socrates for this very wavering between a tolerant and a restrictive point of view. Socrates also gives clear expression to the fact that the vacillation depends on the dualistic complex.

Although Plato mainly discusses what logicians nowadays call one-place predicates (property words), such as:

(I) a is a man
      a is good,

he also considers, at least in passing, two-place predicates (relation expressions), such as:

(II) a and b are two
      a is as large as b
      a is larger than b
      a is identical with b
      a is distinct from b
      a is similar to b

Without explaining his views in detail, he seems to have thought that what holds for (I) holds also for (II), with the necessary modifications.

Plato's "Ideas" are not concepts or thoughts, if by a concept or thought is meant something mental, a perception in the mind. He conceived of ideas as abstract entities which are objects of our thinking.

13. THE THEORY OF IDEAS AS A SEMANTIC THEORY

Let us consider a sentence such as "Socrates is a man". Everyone is agreed that the word "Socrates" is a name of, or designates, a certain person, thus a particular, existing thing. But what is the status of the word "man"? Does it, too, designate something, or does it not? Plato put this question, and he subscribed to the former option. What then does "man" designate? It seems unreasonable to say that it designates any specific human being, say Socrates or Thales or Pythagoras. Plato claimed that it designates just that entity to which he referred as the Idea of Man. What is true of the word "man" applies also to all other words that can be substituted for the letter '*X*' in the logical axiom schemata. If by "semantics" is meant the study of the relationship between verbal expressions and what they refer to (designate, mean), then this aspect of the theory of Ideas is a semantic theory. In order to understand it better, we shall try to formulate explicitly the several assumptions that Plato made but left in a kind of semi-obscurity.

In our study of Socratic–Platonic conceptual analysis in the next chapter, we shall find that Plato had no well-developed feeling for the ambiguities of everyday speech. In the semantic part of the theory of Ideas his somewhat naïve assumption of the unambiguity of language becomes manifest, but it is possible to adjust a semantics of the Platonic type to the actual ambiguity of language. Let us, however, for the sake of simplicity, assume with Plato that words and phrases are unambiguous within the relevant field of language.

To statements within this field Plato applies a name relation:

a is the name of *b*

concerning which he appears to assume:

Axiom schema IV: The expression "*X*(-ness)" is a name of the idea of *X*-ness and nothing else.

Particular axioms exemplifying this schema are obtained by substituting suitable words for '*X*'. The words that may be substituted here are precisely the same as those that may be substituted in the logical schemata. Thus, an axiom covered by IV is 'The expression "man" is a name of the Idea of Man and of nothing else'.

In addition to this "name"-relation Plato also uses another semantic relationship:

a is called "*X*"

concerning which he makes the following assumption:

Axiom schema V: *a* is called "*X*" if and only if *a* partakes of the idea of *X*-ness.

Here, too, the possible substituends for the letter "*X*" are the same as in the logical schemata. A special axiom which comes under V is '*a* is called "man" if and only if *a* partakes of the Idea of Man'.

The import of these semantic axioms may become clearer when some of their obvious corollaries are deduced:

Corollary C: The sentence "*a* is *X*" is true if and only if the thing which the expression "*a*" names partakes of the Idea which the expression "*X*" names.

When Plato speaks of an object *a* being called "*X*", he obviously means that *a* is called "*X*" with truth. An object *a* being called "*X*" with truth is surely the same as the sentence "*a* is *X*" being true.

Corollary D: If the sentence "*a* is *X*" is true, then the entity that "*a*" names is distinct from the entity that "*X*" names.

This corollary follows immediately from the combination of corollary *C* and the logical schema III.

Plato's semantic assumptions have a close kinship to "semantic rules" included in some modern semantic theories. If the mention of "Ideas" is replaced by the mention of "sets" or "properties", Plato's semantic theory may appear extremely trivial. The medieval nominalists, with Ockham in the fore, are to be credited for having shown that Platonic semantics is actually far from trivial.

14. THE THEORY OF IDEAS AS PSYCHOLOGY AND EPISTEMOLOGY

The Ideas, according to Plato, are something we "see" with our reason. This seeing of the Ideas is like the seeing of things with the eyes. Just as we can see an object more or less clearly with our eyes, so can we see an Idea more or less clearly with our reason. According to one opinion of Plato's it is impossible to see Ideas with perfect clarity as long as the soul is united to the body. Plato's theory on the rational seeing of Ideas has both a psychological and an epistemological aspect.

The theory contains the psychological assertion that along with concrete experiential contents such as visual images, for example, there exist abstract contents such as 'manhood', 'horsehood', 'goodness', etc. This view has had a marked influence on philosophical psychology, up to our own time. The rationalists of the modern age, Descartes, Leibniz, and others, have in general accepted the view, whereas empiricists like Locke, Berkeley, Hume, and lately, for example, Carnap, have on the whole rejected it.

What observation by means of the senses is for our knowledge of the sensible world, the seeing by means of reason is for our knowledge of the Ideas. Just as we can describe what we see with our eyes, we can describe what we see with our reason. According to Plato the philosophical sciences, dialectics and pure mathematics, are such descriptions of things seen by reason. Also, the epistemological aspect of Plato's theory has had an influence which can hardly be exaggerated. Even today Platonists and anti-Platonists argue with each other in discussions on the foundations of mathematics and logic.

15. THE THEORY OF IDEAS AS METAPHYSICS

Plato did not stop at the logico-semantic and psychologico-epistemological assumptions recorded above. Through a number of further assumptions his theory of Ideas was transformed into a stimulating but obscure and somewhat incoherent metaphysical theory. It is customary to look upon Plato as an "idealist", in the popular sense of the word. The semantic and logical postulates have no especially "idealistic" meaning, in *this* popular sense, and the same is true of the psychological and epistemological part of Plato's theory. When today Plato is hailed as an "idealist", in the popular sense, it is largely his metaphysics that earns him the attribution. Plato chose to set forth his metaphysical ideas in a metaphorical, poetic idiom, which perhaps shows that he considered them as fancies or as vague inklings of the truth rather than as precise theories. In the *Seventh Letter* he says that he has never written down his deepest philosophy, a truth which cannot be communicated by words but which reveals itself to the select after long contemplation. In any event, this is a warning to his readers not to take him too literally. The readers of the present book should keep this warning in mind, too, when perusing the following summary —the dry bones—of the Platonic metaphysics.

A. Ideas are unchangeable and eternal.

Whereas what today is a couch may tomorrow be a pile of wood, the Idea of Couch itself, the nature common to all couches, cannot undergo any corresponding change; it is and always will remain the same Idea, the same nature, and it exists eternally.

B. Ideas do not exist in space.

In space we come across particular couches, but the Idea of Couch itself, the couch nature, is not to be found there. The Ideas have their home in "a place above the heavens".

C. Ideas are ideal models of which particular things are imperfect copies.

The Idea of the Good is a perfect goodness or something perfectly good; good things in the world of the senses are only more or less good and thus imperfect copies of this perfect goodness. The Idea of Beauty is a perfect beauty which is never more than incompletely realized in the sensible world. The Idea of a Circle is the perfect mathematical circle of which the circles of our world, wagon wheels, bracelets, and planetary orbits, are merely approximations.

D. Ideas are, in one way or another, at least contributory causes of what happens in the material world.

According to a view of Plato's, an object becomes white, for example, when the Idea of the White comes to it, and it ceases to be white when the same Idea departs from it.

E. Ideas form a hierarchical order. The highest idea is the Idea of the Good, which in the world of Ideas plays a role comparable to that of the sun in the world of the senses.

F. Ideas are more real than the things of the sensible world.

The things in the world of the senses are created at one instant and destroyed at another, and while they exist they undergo all sorts of changes. At one instant it is true of a couch that it *is*, and at another instant it is true that it *is not*: at one time it *is* new and complete, at another it *is not* so any longer. Acccording to Plato, this means that the things of the senses, as he says, waver between being and non-being: they are not wholly real. Through their eternity and changelessness the Ideas, on the contrary, possess complete reality.

G. Ideas are more valuable than the things of the sensible world.

In many different ways Plato gives expression to the opinion that the Ideas form a higher and better reality than do the things of the sensible world. Truly good and wise people must long to get away from the world of the senses and to obtain immediate contact with the Ideas.

H. In this life we can only dimly understand the true nature of the Ideas.

Our knowledge of them now is a recollection from the time before birth when we saw them directly with the eyes of the soul, and thereafter we may again be confronted with them face to face.

This metaphysical theory led to difficulties which Plato himself pointed out in the *Parmenides*. This is especially true of assumption C, which, in combination with what I have stated as the third logical axiom of the theory of Ideas, gives rise to a direct contradiction.[8] Some of the objections raised

[8] Let us consider the Idea of Greatness, for example. By the logical axiom schema I:

  (i) Being great is the same as partaking of the Idea of Greatness.

By the third logical axiom:

  (ii) The Idea of Greatness is distinct from anything (*X*) that partakes of that Idea.

If we apply this to the case where *X* is the Idea of Greatness, we get:

in the *Parmenides* were repeated by Aristotle, who revised the theory of Ideas so as to make it immune to them.

Seen from a human angle, Plato's metaphysics has a double aspect. In it Plato expresses his scorn for all that he despised —the sensible world and the people of the sensible world, people who devote themselves to providing comforts for the body, and who consider it worth while to investigate the world of the senses. Plato's metaphysics is also an expression of his discomfort in the world and his ascetic, contemplative longing for something quite different. It seems that the Platonic theory implies also an enormous self-esteem: the noblest thing that man can do is to study the Ideas, and Plato is the first (with the possible exception of Socrates) who even dreamed of their existence. It is a very rich and

(iii) If the Idea of Greatness partakes of itself, it is not identical with itself, which is a *reductio ad absurdum* of the assumption that the Idea of Greatness partakes of itself. Hence:

(iv) The Idea of Greatness does not partake of itself.

From (i) and (iv) we may infer:

(v) The Idea of Greatness is not great.

But the metaphysical assumption C implies the opposite, viz.:

(vi) The Idea of Greatness is great.

and we thus get a contradiction.

The argument in the *Parmenides* is, however, more roundabout. There, the existence of an infinite sequence of Ideas of Greatness is deduced from assumption C. The core of the *Parmenides* argument can, I think, be explained in the following manner. Assume:

(a) S is a set of great things.

Then, by axiom schema I of the Platonic logic, we know:

(b)   All elements of S partake of the Idea of Greatness.

(b)   All elements of S partake of a common idea G.

(c) G is the Idea of Greatness.

By the logical axiom III we get:

(d) G is not an element of S.

By (c) and the metaphysical assumption C we find:

(e) G is something great.

We can now form a new set S' satisfying the condition:

(f) S' consists of all the elements of S and, in addition, G.

Again we have:

(g)   All the elements of S' are great.

(h)   All the elements of S' partake of a common idea G'.

(i) G' is not an element of S'.

In particular:

(j) G' is not identical with G.

Continuing the reasoning in the same way, we may indefinitely prolong the sequence of sets, $S, S', S'' \ldots$, and the corresponding sequence of Ideas, $G, G', G'' \ldots$ All these Ideas will be distinct from one another, and so, Parmenides concludes, we get an infinite number of Ideas of Greatness.

complex personality that speaks to us through the Platonic dialogues, a personality filled with conflicting impulses. The Platonic metaphysics gives expression to only one side of Plato's character. Plato, the very active political theorist, displayed an interest in the affairs of the world which agrees poorly with his conviction that it wavers between being and non-being.

16. PLATO'S PHILOSOPHY OF SCIENCE

Plato assumed a ranking order among the various sciences. The highest place is accorded to the science of Ideas, "dialectics", next comes pure mathematics (pure arithmetic and pure geometry), and last natural science. Plato here presupposes a definite scientific ideal, and the nearer a science comes to this ideal, the higher he ranks it.

A. *Plato's ideal of science*

A science S realizes the Platonic scientific ideal if and only if it simultaneously fulfils the following conditions:

(a) S is a class of absolute truths;

(b) S contains a starting-point, which is characterized by self-evidence and from which all the truths of S can be deduced;

(c) S deals exclusively with the eternal and unchangeable.

According to Plato's own conception, condition (c) is a corollary of (a); for him absolute truths exist only concerning what is eternal and unchangeable. In Plato's system of the sciences there is only one science that completely conforms to the ideal, namely:

B. *Dialectics*

In dialectic thinking there are two roads, the "way upwards", which is of a preparatory character, and the "way downwards", which is the apex of wisdom. When we engage on the upward road, we first consider the particular things of the sensible world. By classifying them we become aware of the specific Ideas under which they fall. These specific Ideas are then grouped under their respective generic Ideas, and thus we ascend step by step, within the system of Ideas, until we finally come face to face with the Idea of the Good. The way downwards is a deductive process which takes its starting-point in the Idea of the Good and then, step by step, develops the lower Ideas. In its downward direction dialectics is a realization, the only one possible, of the ideal of science. Its truths are absolute; the Idea of the Good is an evident starting-point for the deduction of its truths, and they all deal exclusively with what is eternal and unchangeable.

Even though Plato no doubt thought that he gave various samples of dialectic arguments in the dialogues, he probably considered dialectics, the "noblest", the "divine" science, essentially as a dream of the future. He can hardly have formed any very precise notions concerning what it should one day comprise. In any event he did not succeed in conveying such notions to his readers. It seems highly probable, however, that he would have accepted the formal logic framed by Aristotle as a part of the divine science. It also appears likely that Plato's efforts to create dialectics stimulated Aristotle to his work in formal logic. Plato's dialectical arguments are largely concerned with ethical problems. It is perhaps not too rash to assume that Platonic dialectics in its finished state was intended to include ethics in so far as ethics sets forth definitions and perhaps also certain general norms. Plato also considered the axioms of mathematics to be deducible within dialectics, and he thought it an important scientific task to carry out this deduction.

If we keep in mind Plato's belief that dialectics and mathematics exhaust the realm of the eternal and unchangeable (cf. the *Republic*, book VI) and that the axioms of mathematics are provable within dialectics, we see that dialectics, as Plato conceived it, assumes the form of a universal rational science. It becomes a complete theory of the eternal and unchanging. This property of dialectics should possibly be reckoned as a constituent of what I have called above the Platonic ideal of science. If so, then to conditions (a)–(c) should be added the following:

    (d) *S* contains among its conclusions *all* "absolute" truths, all truths about the eternal and unchanging.

C. *Pure mathematics*

According to Plato, pure mathematics does not realize what I have called the Platonic ideal of science, but it comes closer to the ideal than natural science does. Plato's views in this respect can, I think, be summarized by saying that pure mathematics (a) is a class of absolute truths, (b) has a point of departure, its axioms and definitions, from which all its truths can be rigorously deduced, and (c) deals exclusively with the eternal and unchangeable, but that (b') its point of departure does *not* exhibit the self-evidence that the ideal requires. So long as the mathematical axioms have not been proved—and the mathematician as such cannot prove them, since they are the starting-point for all his proofs—pure mathematics is left hanging in the air according to Plato. It is "like a dream" he says.[9] It needs for its complement dialectics, which is assumed to have other possibilities of proof at its disposal. Mathematics achieves the status of perfect knowledge only when the mathematical axioms have been developed from the Idea of the Good on the downward road of dialectics.

Plato's conception of the objects of mathematics is interesting enough to merit a more detailed account. There exist mathematical Ideas just as well as other kinds of Idea. The Idea of the number One, the number Two, the number Three, etc., are Ideas of which every set containing one, two, three, etc., elements, partakes. In geometry there occur such Ideas as those of the Straight Line, the Circle, the Diagonal, the Square, etc. Besides these Ideas, however, mathematicians also contemplate another kind of entity which is accessible only to thought. There exist infinitely many abstract arithmetical "units" (monads). When, without reference to sensible objects, the arithmetician says that $2 + 3 = 5$, he is thinking of sets of these units, and his meaning is that a two-element set conjoined with a disjoint three-element set gives a five-element set as a result. There exists also a world of geometric figures accessible only to thought. When the geometer mentally "conjoins" two points with a straight line, for example, it is such geometrical entities that he is

---

[9] Plato, *Republic*, 533 b, c.

considering. These arithmetic units and geometric figures are as unchangeable, as eternal, as are the Ideas. When mathematicians speak as if they carried out operations upon these objects—"adding" two numbers, "joining" two points, etc.—they are guilty of a misleading manner of speech. They can in no way influence the objects of mathematics, they can merely observe them and systematically formulate their observations.

D. *Natural science*

In section 7C, we saw that Plato's attitude to natural science was marked by a profound scepticism.

The unchanging and eternal alone is real in the complete sense: only this really *is*. Because of its changeability, the sensible world wavers between being and non-being and thereby fails to be fully real. Exact knowledge about the sensible world is therefore impossible. One can form an "opinion" (*doxa*) about it but not have exact "knowledge" (*noesis*). Mathematical natural science is no exception to this. Astronomy describes the orbits of the heavenly bodies by means of geometric curves such as circles and spirals. Such a description is never more than approximately correct, since perfect mathematical circles and spirals are not found in nature. In the study of nature it is thus impossible to achieve the ideal of science, and the philosopher who seeks wisdom can never whole-heartedly devote himself to empirical investigations.

E. *The Platonic problem in astronomy*

Although Plato's attitude to natural science was in the main negative, he must be credited with an important positive contribution. His statement of a problem in astronomy dominated the efforts of astronomers for almost 2,000 years and in due time inspired Kepler to his formulation of the planetary laws.

The sun, the moon, and the planets apparently move in extremely intricate and irregular paths across the heavens. For Plato, the dualist, however, the heavenly bodies are all divine beings. A divine being, like a respectable citizen, should move about in an orderly manner. In other words, the true motions of these bodies must be quite different from their apparent motions. The only motion becoming to a god is the uniform circular one. For this reason, Plato gave the mathematicians and astronomers of his time the task of constructing a mathematical theory that would describe the true motions of the sun, the moon, and the planets in terms of uniform circular motion, and would explain the apparent motions as projections of the true ones upon the heavens. To carry out this task successfully would be, Plato said, "to save phenomena".

A geocentric, orthodox Platonic solution of this problem was given by Plato's pupils Eudoxus and Calippus (fourth century BC) and further developed by Aristotle. Two other solutions, also geocentric but perhaps less strictly Platonic, were given by Hipparchus of Rhodes and by Ptolemy of Alexandria (second century BC). Aristarchus of Samos (third century BC) had already shown, in principle, how phenomena could be saved by means of a heliocentric theory, but not until the seventeenth century did the heliocentric conception prevail, thanks to the works of Copernicus and Kepler.

F. *The Platonic philosophy of science in later times*

Plato's philosophy of science has left deep traces in the entire culture of the West. His idea of science was made more precise by his pupil, Aristotle. This sharpening was so significant and illuminating that it is historically justified to speak of the Platonic–Aristotelian ideal of science. It inspired the Greek mathematicians, and Euclid's *Elements* was conceived under its influence. Its offshoot, the axiomatic method, plays a vital part in the formal sciences of today. In philosophy it had a renaissance in the seventeenth century among the rationalistic philosophers (Descartes, Spinoza, Leibniz).

Several different trains of thought are combined in Plato's ideal of science. With the requirement of an axiomatic or deductive construction of science he conjoined the demand that the axioms should have the epistemological quality of self-evidence or obvious certainty. Plato was probably the first to introduce this unrealistic and disastrous requirement into philosophy. It has been a dominant motive through the entire history of philosophy, and even today there are philosophers who find it difficult to free themselves from it. The combination of these two conditions, axiomatic construction and self-evidence in the axioms, reappears in Aristotle and also in the seventeenth-century rationalists.

Using a modern jargon, we may say that on Plato's view all genuinely scientific truths must be *a priori* (independent of experience). In his philosophy of science Plato gives his answers to three different questions about *a priori* knowledge: (i) What is its scope? Plato's answer was: "Dialectics" (probably including ethics and logic) and mathematics (identified with arithmetic and geometry). (ii) Is it axiomatizable? His reply was affirmative. (iii) From what system of axioms can it be deduced? Plato answered, deplorably vaguely, by pointing to the Idea of the Good. Concerning (ii), most subsequent adherents to the Platonic–Aristotelian ideal of science have been in agreement with Plato. It was left to modern logic to bring about a serious reconsideration of his answer to (ii): it has shown that not even arithmetic is axiomatizable. On questions (i) and (iii) opinions have varied widely in the course of time.

Plato's philosophy of science set off a long development of thought which is in part a chapter in the history of human errors, but which has also led to valuable insights into the nature of axiomatic systems and formalized axiomatic systems. It has also shed some light upon the distinction between *a priori* and *a posteriori* knowledge and between truths of reason ("eternal", "necessary", "analytic" truths) and experimental truths ("factual", "contingent", "synthetic" truths).

In the logicist deduction of arithmetic, which was achieved by Frege and Russell, it is possible to see a realization of Plato's demand for a "dialectic" proof of the axioms of mathematics. Of course we do not know whether Plato himself would have looked upon the logicist theory in this way, had it been brought to his attention.[10] The order of rank

[10] The logicist interpretation of arithmetic adduced by Frege and Russell is also reminiscent of Plato in other respects. Both were influenced by Cantor's set theory and believed, like Plato, but unlike Aristotle, in the existence of an actual infinite in mathematics (concerning this notion, cf. §20 below). Also, their view on the nature of cardinal numbers offers a striking resemblance to Plato's interpretation of the integers as Ideas.

which Plato established between the purely conceptual sciences (dialectics and mathematics) and the natural sciences may well have encouraged the Greek mathematicians. But it can also have been one of the many reasons why the Greeks never achieved as much in the natural sciences as they did in pure mathematics. Plato's judgement was accepted by the fathers of the Christian church, and part of the responsibility for the decline of science during the Middle Ages indirectly lies with him.

17. PLATO'S VIEWS ON MAN AND THE WORLD

Like Empedocles and the Pythagoreans, whose views influenced him, Plato supposed that the soul is only temporarily joined to the body. It existed before it became united with the body at birth, and it is going to survive the body's death. The soul is related to the eternal Ideas, to which it is attracted by a transcendental love (*eros*). Since the body and its senses are an obstacle to the philosopher in his attempts to obtain a clear view of the Ideas, he must welcome deliverance from the body, i.e. death. In a series of myths Plato has described the transmigration of the soul and the judgement it must undergo in the beyond. The notion that the mental functions are tied to an entity, the soul, which is different in principle from the body and is capable of existing independently, may be called the Platonic concept of soul. This concept, which is conspicuously absent from the Bible, was borrowed from Plato by the Church fathers and incorporated into the Christian doctrinal system. In the seventeenth century it was given its clearest formulation in Descartes' theory of the soul as a *substantia cogitans* (thinking substance) in contrast to the body as a *substantia extensa* (extended substance).

The only real evil that may befall man is his own "injustice". Injustice is a disharmony or a disease of the soul which it is incumbent upon us to save it from. In this respect, too, the Christian theologians were to recognize their own thoughts in Plato.

The world as described in the *Timaeus* (cf. §7A) is the well-ordered home of men and gods. Nature must be explained in such a manner that its order is seen to be the best that is possible. The world has been formed by the Demiurge as a great organism whose constitution is purposeful in all respects and which is governed by a world-soul. Man, too, who is a miniature image of the world, is framed so as to function as well as possible.

Plato accepted the geocentric astronomical theory proposed by his pupil Eudoxus, but gave it a theological interpretation. The fixed stars, the planets, the sun, the moon, and also the earth, are divine beings. Each soul has originally descended to earth from its particular star, and when transmigration comes to an end, it will return thither.

The stars influence the happenings on earth through their positions in the sky. Periodically all the heavenly bodies reappear in exactly the same positions and this periodicity is reflected in the happenings on earth, including human affairs.

The world of the *Timaeus* has a pronounced anthropocentric, teleological, and theological character.

III

The Methods of Science

18. ARISTOTLE

Aristotle (384–322 BC), who was born in the city of Stagira in Northern Greece, went as a youth to Athens to study. There he joined the Academy, which was then led by Plato. After a period of scientific activity in Asia Minor, he was for years the teacher of the Macedonian crown prince, the future Alexander the Great. In the year 355 BC he founded his own school in Athens—the Lykeion, also called the "Peripatetic" school—to which he devoted the rest of his life. The school survived until about AD 200. There he lectured on most of the philosophical and scientific disciplines known at the time. His many extant writings are thought to be the incompletely organized or imperfectly edited notes for his lectures.

At the beginning of his scientific career, Aristotle seems to have been a faithful and enthusiastic Platonist. In time, his outlook grew more independent, and he was to level sharp criticism against many points in Plato's philosophy. Nevertheless, his definitive philosophy appears as a modification and development of Plato's. What most truly distinguishes the mature Aristotle from Plato, and has often caused them to be considered opposite philosophical types, is a difference in temperament and interests. Whereas Plato scorned the world of the senses and its study, Aristotle had an encyclopedic interest in, and a deep respect for, empirical facts. While Plato, in poetic metaphor, praised the world of Ideas and the soul which longs to be with them, Aristotle speaks in the sober language of the scientist throughout his preserved writings.

Aristotle's modifications of Plato's theory of Ideas consist mainly in his pruning away most of the metaphysical superstructure (§ 19). In the same spirit he also refashioned Plato's theory of the objects of pure mathematics (§ 20). Inspired by Plato's ideal of science, he developed a methodology of the deductive sciences (§21) and a formal deductive logic (§30), both of which were epoch-making in the development of scientific thought. Aristotle's efforts were to a great extent directed towards creating the conceptual apparatus that future research would use (§22). Such an attempt may be judged naïve on the ground that it cannot readily be known what concepts are fruitful until they are actually applied to the data of experience. The *naïveté*, however, resided more in those who, during the Middle Ages and the Renaissance, dogmatically held to the Aristotelian framework of concepts, than in the originator himself, who here, as always, argued in a searching and experimental spirit. The Aristotelian analysis of concepts will be taken up in Chapter IV, where it will be studied in its relationship to the thoughts of Socrates and Plato in the same field.

19. CRITIQUE OF THE THEORY OF IDEAS

A. *Critique of the metaphysical aspect of the theory of Ideas*

Despite his various reservations and somewhat different terminology, Aristotle seems to have accepted what I have called the logical and semantic aspects of Plato's theory of Ideas. A word that we may predicate of a number of individual objects designates an Idea (*eidos, genos*) or a Form (*morphe*). It is, or used to be, customary to translate the same Greek word by "Idea" when it appears in Plato and by "Form" when it appears in Aristotle. This rather arbitrary tradition has been instrumental in obscuring the highly important agreement that exists between Plato's and Aristotle's views. The psychological and epistemological parts of the theory of Ideas also reappear in Aristotle with certain modifications (which may be bypassed here). He too countenanced abstract content of experience along with the concrete contents. What Aristotle objected to in Plato's theory was mainly the metaphysical assumptions with which Plato burdened it. In opposition to Plato, Aristotle asserted:

I. Forms (Ideas) are not ideal models or archetypes of which individual objects are imperfect replicas.

Plato's contrary assumption is at variance with the basic intention of the theory of Ideas. The Idea of Man, for example, is supposed to be the nature or form that is characteristic of all men. If we now say that this Idea is an ideal image, the perfect man, we assume that it is a man. The nature that characterizes everything that is a man cannot, however, itself be a man. In other words, the property of being a man does not possess that very property.

Aristotle mentions that Plato's opposite assumption gives rise to an absurdity known as "the third man". Apparently he is here referring to the line of reasoning that Plato himself presented in the *Parmenides*.

II. Forms (Ideas) do not exist in the abstract (or in a separate world of Ideas), isolated from individual objects.

Plato's contrary assumption, here too, is at variance with the basic intention of the theory of Ideas. The idea of Man is the nature found in all men. To assert, as Plato does, that it exists in a place beyond the heavens is thus unreasonable.

B. *Substances and universals*

Plato's distinction between the concrete objects given to the senses and the Ideas was modified and sharpened by Aristotle through his distinction between (primary) substances and universals. A (primary) substance, according to Aristotle, is an individual object, such as a human being, a horse, a tree. The following properties are characteristic of such substances:

(1) A substance cannot be predicated of a subject.

We may meaningfully say: "Socrates is (a) man", and thus predicate 'man' of Socrates, but we cannot meaningfully say: "*A* is (a) Socrates", as long as we let "Socrates" be the proper name of a man.

(2) A substance is something that we can point out as a "this".

(3) A substance can change its properties without losing its identity. The same person can be at one time white, at another black.

(4) Only substances exist in a primary sense.

If we say, for example, that the nature of 'man' exists, this means that there exist substances in which this nature occurs.

If substances did not exist, nothing at all would exist.

That which is not a substance is a universal, something that can be predicated of something. Aristotle distinguished between various categories of universals. Some universals are species and genera (secondary substances), others are quantities (e.g. 'two feet long'), others qualities (e.g. 'white'), others relations (e.g. 'twice as large'), and so on. Using this terminology, Aristotle formulated point 1 of his critique of the theory of Ideas by saying that Plato incorrectly regarded universals as a kind of substances.

Since the distinction between substance and universal was first introduced by Aristotle, it has played a fundamental role, in one form or another, in practically all subsequent philosophical speculation.

The nominalists of the Middle Ages and of more recent times deny the existence of universals, but thereby presuppose the meaningfulness of the Aristotelian distinction. In modern Anglo-Saxon philosophy, this distinction reappears in the form of the distinction between "particulars (individuals)" and "universals". Unfortunately the meaning of the distinction is not at all as clear as might be expected in view of its frequent use.

20. CRITIQUE OF PLATO'S THEORY OF THE OBJECTS OF PURE MATHEMATICS

According to Plato, the objects of pure mathematics, like the Ideas, exist in isolation from the world of the senses. Aristotle was bound to reject this notion as well. There exist no abstract arithmetical units (monads); the arithmetician only ignores the multiplicity that every counted object comprises, and considers it as a unit. Nor do abstract, "immovable" geometric features exist; the geometer disregards the properties of objects other than their geometric ones, considering them merely as geometric lines, surfaces, or bodies. The mathematician, Aristotle thinks, performs a kind of idealizing abstraction.

A particular consequence of Plato's theory of mathematics is evidently the following, which concerns the concept of the infinite. It is natural for the mathematician to say that given any positive integer n, he can always construct the larger integer $n + 1$. Since the integers have an eternal existence in Plato's theory, the mathematician should, in keeping with his theory, say instead that to any given integer n there exists a larger integer $n + 1$, and hence that there exists an infinite sequence of integers. Analogously, it is natural for a geometer to say that given a line segment AB, he can always extend it to a larger segment CD (see (I)). Since, according

(I)

to Plato's theory, the objects of geometry have an eternal existence, the geometer should, in keeping with this theory, say instead that the segment AB is a part of the longer segment CD, and in fact, that there exist infinite straight lines. If every segment is divisible, as geometry postulates, then also, from the Platonic point of view, every segment contains infinitely many subsegments.

Aristotle protests against this Platonic view of the mathematical infinite. Neither in arithmetic nor in geometry is there an "actual infinity", according to his view. The infinite exists only as a "potentiality". The sequence of integers: 1, 2, 3 . . . is potentially infinite by addition, in the sense that given any integer a larger integer *can* be created by addition. In geometry, for example, a finite segment is potentially infinite by division in the sense that, given a particular division of the segment into a finite number of finite segments, one always *can* effect a finer division of this sort. Although at times Aristotle seems to acknowledge only in geometry this potential infinity by division, on other occasions he states that, given a finite segment, one always *can* construct a longer finite segment that includes the given one.

Some of Aristotle's ideas on the mathematical infinite could perhaps be expressed as follows in modern terminology:

(1) There exists no set containing an infinite number of objects.

By a set of Cs we shall mean a set each of whose members is an instance of the concept C. Let us agree further to say that a set S is a proper subset of the set S' if all the elements of S are elements of S', and moreover S' contains at least one element which does not belong to S. For example, the set $\{2, 3, 4\}$ is a proper subset of the set $\{2, 3, 4, 5\}$. According to Aristotle, certain concepts C are then characterized by a potential infinity in the following sense:

(2) Every finite set of Cs can eventually be made into a proper subset of more comprehensive finite set of Cs.

21. THE METHODOLOGY OF DEMONSTRATIVE SCIENCE

Both Aristotle and Plato considered the demonstrative, or deductive, sciences to be the most perfect, indeed the only true sciences. For Plato the notion of a demonstrative science remained a vision which he succeeded only very imperfectly in translating into intelligible concepts. Aristotle, on the other hand, has left us, in the *Posterior Analytics*, a very elaborate, highly sophisticated, and in parts quite lucid, statement of his conception of demonstrative science. This conception was partly based upon an analysis of the two demonstrative sciences in existence in Aristotle's time, viz. arithmetic and geometry. It was also partly derived from Aristotle's own logical doctrines, his syllogistic and his theory of genera and species, definitions and essences. The existing demonstrative sciences were, as is to be expected, seen by Aristotle through the medium of his own philosophical pre-conceptions. What follows is a very much simplified account of the resulting Aristotelian methodology.

A. *The general logical structure of a demonstrative science*

Some of the conditions that Aristotle expected the logical structure of a demonstrative science to fulfil may be expressed as follows.

(1) There is a finite number of basic propositions which are postulated without proof.

Aristotle did not explicitly say that the basic propositions of a demonstrative science are to be finite in number, but it is clear that this was his intention.

(2) A proposition that is not basic may be asserted if and

only if it has been derived from the basic propositions by logical inference.

Aristotle had himself worked out the logic of one special class of inferences, the so-called syllogisms (cf. Ch. V, § 30). Overestimating the importance of this achievement, he assumed:

(3) The inferences always proceed by means of syllogisms.

Among the syllogisms, he considered those belonging to the so-called first figure to be the scientifically most perfect. As most perfect of all he viewed the syllogism later known as Barbara:

(i)   All b are c
      All a are b
      Hence: All a are c.

This is the only syllogism whose conclusion is both universal and affirmative, and universality is superior to particularity, affirmation to negation. One of Aristotle's characteristic ideas on demonstration can be most easily indicated by considering a demonstration in which every inference is of this type Barbara. Such a demonstration is scientifically complete only if, as Aristotle puts it, it is "close-packed". The inference (i) involves the three kinds a, b, c, and it is asserted in (i) that a is a part of b and b a part of c; we might represent this as follows:

(ii) a part of b part of c.

If (i) belongs to scientific knowledge, its propositions are true and hence (ii) is a fact. Now it may happen that there exists an intermediate kind b' between, say, b and c:

(iii) a part of b part of b' part of c.

Our demonstration is then incomplete unless it justifies the proposition, 'All b are c', by the inference:

(iv)   All b' are c
       All b are b'
       Hence, all b are c.

A demonstration without any such incompleteness is close-packed in Aristotle's sense. He thinks that this notion can be generalized so as to be applicable to demonstrations in general. On his view, between any two kinds *a* and *c* such that *a* is a part of *c* there exist at most a finite number of intermediate kinds *b* such that (ii). From this assumption he can infer that any scientific demonstration can be completed so as to become close-packed, and he demands that it be so:

(4) All scientific demonstrations shall be close-packed.

B. *Truth and necessity*

The propositions of science are objects of knowledge, and knowledge is by its very nature knowledge of truths. Thus Aristotle maintains:

(5) The basic propositions are true.

Since only truths can be inferred from truths, the following is an immediate corollary of (2) and (5):

(6) Any proposition that can be asserted in a demonstrative science is true.

Contingent truth, however, is not enough in the basic propositions. A further demand of Aristotle's is:

(7) The basic propositions must be necessary.

Since conclusions from necessary premises are themselves necessary, (7) gives the corollary:

(8) All propositions that can be asserted in a demonstrative science are necessary.

For Aristotle, the necessity of a proposition means that the concepts involved in the proposition are "essentially connected" in the manner the proposition asserts. With regard to the proposition, 'All *a* are *b*', such essential connection obtains, e.g., when *b* is included as an element in the 'essence' of *a*.

C. *Order of derivation and "causal" order*

Besides the notion of syllogistic derivability, Aristotle also employs another notion, expressed by saying that certain true propositions are the "cause" (or "reason" or "ground") of a certain other proposition being true. This notion is stronger than syllogistic derivability: not any syllogism, not even any syllogism all of whose propositions are true, gives the "cause" of, or "reason" for, its conclusion being true.

The syllogism:

> (v) All non-twinkling bodies are near
> The planets are non-twinkling
> Hence, the planets are near

does, e.g., not give us the reason for the proximity of the planets. On the other hand, the syllogism:

> (vi) The planets are near
> Bodies that are near do not twinkle
> Hence, the planets do not twinkle

does afford an insight into the reason for its conclusion.[1] Aristotle maintains:

> (9) The inferences of a demonstrative science must give us the reasons for their conclusions.

In several passages, Aristotle also seems to assert:

> (10) The basic propositions of a demonstrative science are such that no further reasons for them can be adduced.

Aristotle expresses this idea by saying that the basic propositions are "indemonstrable".

D. *Order of derivation and order of knowledge*

We shall now consider Aristotle's thoughts on the relation between the propositions of a demonstrative science and human knowledge. Demonstrative science is the highest form of knowledge. Hence:

> (11) The basic propositions of a demonstrative science are objects of knowledge, and further propositions become known as they are inferred from the basic ones.

---

[1] Aristotle, *Posterior Analytics*, I 13, 78ª 30 ff.

To the logical order in which the propositions are derived in a demonstrative science corresponds an order within our knowledge:

> (12) Our knowledge of the propositions inferred is an effect of our knowledge of the premisses from which they are inferred.

While our knowledge of the conclusions is, in this sense, mediated, our knowledge of the basic propositions is, in a corresponding sense, immediate:

> (13) Our knowledge of the basic propositions is not the effect of a knowledge of any ulterior premisses from which they might be inferred.

Finally, Aristotle thinks that the knowledge of the basic propositions is marked by a superior certainty: they are "better known" than the conclusions; our conviction as to their truth is "unshakable". Perhaps we could express this part of Aristotle's view in the words:

> (14) The basic propositions have an absolute certainty or self-evidence.

Aristotle speaks of a special faculty in the human mind, a rational intuition, by which we become aware of, and convinced of the truth of, the basic propositions. From them certainty spreads downward along the chains of syllogistic argument to the propositions derived.

E. *The homogeneity of a demonstrative science*

An important feature which, in Aristotle's opinion, characterizes demonstrative science is what might be called its homogeneity:

> (15) To each demonstrative science corresponds a unique genus such that all the propositions of the science deal exclusively with objects belonging to that genus; and to different sciences correspond different genera.

When Aristotle speaks here of a genus, he seems to be thinking of a class pertaining to the natural system of classification that he presumes. Exactly how Aristotle conceives the relation between a science and its genus is not clear. However, he exemplifies the idea by saying that units and numbers are the genus of arithmetic, geometrical figures the genus of geometry.

In keeping with (15), Aristotle maintained that geometric theorems cannot be proved in arithmetic, and arithmetical theorems cannot be proved in geometry.

F. *The system of the sciences*

Aristotle explicitly recognized three sciences which he considered capable of being put into a form satisfying his demands upon a demonstrative (theoretical) science. They are:

(1) first philosophy
(2) mathematics
(3) physics.

According to one definition, Aristotle's first philosophy, or, as it is now usually called, his metaphysics, is concerned with "being as being". When Aristotle adduces the law of contraction and the law of the excluded middle as examples of metaphysical principles, it might be supposed that the science of being as being is a sort of logic. In other contexts, however, Aristotle identifies the first philosophy with theology. In mathematics Aristotle distinguishes on the one hand between (2a) a universal mathematics whose propositions hold for 'magnitudes' in general, regardless of whether they are numbers, or line segments, or surfaces, or volumes, or intervals of time, or something else, and on the other hand the special disciplines such as (2b) arithmetic and (2c) geometry.

According to one notion of Aristotle's, the sequence of sciences, (3)–(2)–(1), is characterized by successively increasing abstraction. Physics (3) studies nature in general, and especially bodies in their motion. Mathematics (2) abstracts from all properties of natural phenomena except the quantitative. In particular, it abstracts from motion, and in this sense its objects may be said to be unmoved. The first philosophy (1) disregards all properties of things other than precisely their being. The sequence (3)–(2)–(1) can be completed by taking into consideration the different disciplines of mathematics. The sequence (3)–(2c)–(2b)–(2a)–(1) is also characterized by increasing abstraction. Geometry (2c) disregards all properties of bodies other than the geometrical ones. Arithmetic (2b) disregards the geometrical ones also and considers bodies merely as units.

In the reversed sequence, (1)–(2a)–(2b)–(2c)–(3), each subsequent member is obtained from its predecessor by the addition of new basic assumptions. The first philosophy, according to an idea of Aristotle's, rests solely upon such very general assumptions as have validity for arbitrary types of magnitudes. As a principle of this nature, Aristotle mentions the proposition that if a and b are magnitudes of the same category, then a is either greater than, or equal to, or less than, b. Arithmetic then adduces further assumptions which hold for the sequence of integers 1, 2, 3 . . . And so on. Oddly enough, formal logic, whose father we usually see Aristotle as being, has not been allotted any place in his system of demonstrative sciences.

G. *The role of induction in demonstrative science*

When Aristotle speaks of "induction" (*epagoge*), he sometimes seems to think of deductive reasonings of the form:

a_1 is B

$\vdots$

a_n is B
$a_1 \ldots a_n$ are all the A
Hence, all A are B

or the form:

All A_1 are B

$\vdots$

All A_n are B
All A are either A_1, or . . . or A_n
Hence, all A are B.

In some passages, he also shows awareness of what we today call induction, viz. inferences from 'all known' to 'all'. The type of 'induction', however, to which Aristotle attributes a really important role in his theory of demonstrative science is what is nowadays sometimes referred to as 'intuitive induction'. By considering a number of particular *A*s that are *B*, we come to perceive the universal connection between *A* and *B*: 'All *A* are *B*'. When we have once, through *epagoge*, become aware of the connection, it becomes the object of a rational intuition. It is in this manner that we come to know the basic propositions of the demonstrative sciences.

22. THE PRINCIPLES OF SCIENTIFIC EXPLANATION

Although Aristotle shared Plato's partiality for the deductive sciences, unlike Plato he had a passionate interest in empirical research. He holds a prominent position in the early history of many empirical sciences, e.g. astronomy, mechanics, biology, psychology, and politics. His works on biology are filled with exact observations which aroused the admiration even of Darwin. He also thought deeply, though not always successfully, about the methods by which scientific explanation is to be achieved. Let us see what he thought about certain problems that come under this heading.

A. *Why does an acorn grow to be an oak, but not a maple?*

How is it that a hen's egg becomes a chicken, but never an elephant? Aristotle thinks that it depends upon the potential properties of the acorn or the egg. Potentially, albeit not actually, the acorn is already an oak, and the egg is already a chicken. On the other hand, the acorn is not potentially a maple, and the egg is not potentially an elephant. All development consists in some potentiality (*dynamis*) being transformed into actuality (*energeia*). The width of possible development of an object is thus the same as the width of its potential properties.

If we accept the definitions:

   (i) *a* has the property *E* actually = Df *a* has *E*

   (ii) *a* has the property *E* potentially = Df *a* can come to have *E* actually,

Aristotle's view, mentioned above, merely restates what is already implied by the concepts of actuality and potentiality. The view is thus incontrovertible but, alas, also trivial. It often led to fruitless sophistry in later science for the simple reason that its triviality was overlooked. As we shall soon see, Aristotle himself did not consistently stick to the interpretation of the terms codified by definitions (i) and (ii).

B. *Why does each element move towards its natural place?*

Aristotle believed that each of the four elements: earth, water, air, and fire, has its natural place, as indicated in diagram (J). The ether is a fifth element which Aristotle assumed to fill the space beyond the orbit of the moon in

(J)

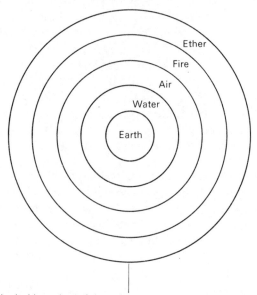

The spherical boundary of the universe

which the sun and the planets revolve. According to Aristotle, if an element is not impelled by an external force to move differently, it will move towards its natural place. This natural direction of motion cannot, he thought, be explained otherwise than by assuming that each element has an inherent tendency to move towards its natural place. He also said that each element potentially occupies its natural place, and that its natural motion is an actualization of this potentiality. The potential emerges here, not only as that which can be actualized, but also as that which strives to become actualized.

C. *Why does a stone continue to move through the air after it has been thrown from the hand?*

The modern explanation of this fact appeals to the law of inertia, which states that a body not influenced by an exterior force either remains at rest or continues with constant speed in the line of its direction of motion. Time after time Aristotle came close to an idea very similar to this law, but in the end he rejected it as physically irrelevant because it concerns a situation that never occurs in nature. Instead, he asserted that the stone moves forward only as long as it is in direct contact with some other body which is pressing it on. In the present case, Aristotle believed that the other body can be identified with that part of the air through which the stone moves. In general, he considered that a body B moves only as long as a second body or force A keeps it in motion. If a body B is in motion at an instant t, the question is always pertinent: What body or force A keeps B in motion at t? In answering this question, Aristotle could sometimes resort to hypotheses which fall within the bounds of what is empirically observable, as in the case of the stone's flight. His theory became more difficult to sustain with regard to the motions of the heavenly bodies. Aristotle was forced here to employ hypotheses of a partly theological character. The heavenly bodies are attached to spheres formed of some divine matter which our senses are too gross to perceive. It is these spheres, rotating in a complex fashion, that keep the heavenly bodies in motion. The spheres in turn obtain their motion from certain intelligences, each of which is responsible for the revolution of its particular sphere. The supreme among these intelligences, the "unmoved mover", or God, holds the sphere of the fixed stars in rotation.

D. *What are the causes of any given process?*

The goal of science is to discover causes (origins, *aitia*) and in each individual case four different types of interacting causes must be taken into consideration. Let us suppose that a sculptor transforms a block of marble into a statue. The material cause of the statue is the marble. Another cause is the formal cause, which is here the geometrical form of the finished statue. A third cause is the effective cause, which by its activity gives rise to the transformation, in this case the sculptor. The fourth cause is the final cause, the sculptor's purpose in carving the block.

The sculptor has in mind a certain purpose which guides him in his work. Aristotle thinks that nature herself also works towards a goal:

Nature is like a good housekeeper who never throws away anything that might be put to some use.[2]

Nature behaves as if it foresaw the future.[3]

Aristotle refers to the goals of nature especially when discussing biological problems. He distinguishes between those characteristics that are common to all normal members of a biological species and those that are found only in some of its members. The common characteristics, he thinks, are to be explained essentially as the result of final causes, whereas effective causes are mainly responsible for the individual variations. The purpose to which he refers is the perpetuation of each species by properly functioning individuals. Empedocles' attempt to explain existing species by means of natural selection was rejected by Aristotle as unsatisfactory.

E. *Form and matter*

The terms 'form' (*eidos*) and 'matter' (*hyle*) occupy a prominent place in the expression of Aristotle's ideas. He uses these terms in two different grammatical ways, in contexts of the type:

(i)   *a* is the form of *b*
      b is the matter of *a*

as well as in those of the type:

(ii)   *a* is form
       b is matter.

The two statements under (i) signify the same. The statements of type (ii) can plausibly be reduced to those of type (i) by the definitions:

---

[2] Aristotle, *De Generatione Animalium*, II 6, 744[b] 16 f.
[3] Aristotle, *De Caelo*, II 9, 291[a] 24 f.

a is form = Df There is a *b* such that *a* is the form of *b*;

a is matter = Df There is a *b* such that *b* is the form of *a*.

What Aristotle calls "pure form" and "first matter" can apparently be defined as follows:

a is pure form = Df *a* is form, and *a* is not matter;

a is first matter = Df *a* is matter, and *a* is not form.

But let us leave these subtle exegetical questions unsettled.

Let us consider instead some of Aristotle's statements of type (i). 'First matter' is matter relative to the quality pairs, wet–dry, cold–warm, of the four classical elements. The four elements are the matter of all compound substances occurring in nature. The element copper is matter relative to the form of a copper bowl. The human body is the matter of its soul. In a definition, the *genus proximum* is the matter of the *differentia specifica*. Aristotle assumed that the entire universe constitutes a hierarchy ordered by the relation between matter and form. The base of this hierarchy is the first matter and its summit is God who is pure form. It is certainly difficult to discern an interesting common relationship in the pairs of objects on which Aristotle sets the stamp of matter and form.

23. ARISTOTLE ON MAN AND THE UNIVERSE

Aristotle's universe, about which something has already been said in §§7B and 22B, is closely similar to the universe of Plato's *Timaeus.* They are both spheres with the earth in the centre and the heavens as boundary. In both the heavenly phenomena are of a divine nature. Plato speaks as if the world had been formed by the Demiurge, but how seriously are his words to be taken here? Aristotle leaves us in no doubt that his universe has always been and will always be. The heavenly bodies pursue their courses, from eternity and into eternity, periodically repeating the same constellations. The eternal recurrence of the constellations brings with it the eternal recurrence of those great events on earth that are caused by the stars.

Contrary to Plato, Aristotle did not assume that body and soul in man are two distinct things, two substances, only contingently united during life on earth. The animated body is a single substance, in which we can distinguish between the body and the soul only in the same sense that we can distinguish between the wax and its form in a piece of wax. The soul, therefore, cannot be supposed to survive the body. Along with the Platonic concept of the soul, the Aristotelian concept thereof as a "form" of the body takes its place as one of the great classical attempts to explain the relationship between mind and body. Aristotle's theory is not completely free from ambiguity, however. The human soul is composed of a nutritive soul, whose functions are the ingestion of nourishment and procreation, an animal soul, which is a soul of perception, memory, and imagination, and finally a rational soul, by which we think and which distinguishes man from plants and animals. It is by means of the rational soul that we intuitively grasp the basic assumptions of the deductive sciences and make inferences from them. The highest part of the rational soul is something that Aristotle calls the active reason. Through this active reason we partake of immortality. The ambiguity of Aristotle's theory about the soul and its immortality gave rise to spirited discussions during the Middle Ages, and also to heresies that the Church saw it as necessary to condemn.

When, in his ethical works, Aristotle described what he considered to be the good life, he had in mind only the free citizen of a Greek city state. He never questioned the institution of slavery, and he never dreamt of granting the slaves a right to the good life also. The free citizen's good life, as depicted by Aristotle, is, on the whole, a very well-balanced life. He lives best who, during a long life, has the opportunity to develop all his human capabilities, who finds in everything the golden mean between the extremes, and who acts with insight into the relevant moral norms, his own personal attitudes, and the meaning of his actions. In his catalogue of the virtues that go into the perfect life, Aristotle includes courage, self-control, friendship, humour, and scientific thinking.

IV

Socratic Concept Analysis and
Platonic – Aristotelian Speculation

24. THE ORIGIN OF CONCEPTUAL ANALYSIS

The investigation of our instruments for describing reality to which Socrates gave the impulse and which was carried out by Plato and Aristotle, was as epoch-making a contribution to the history of thought as the creation of a scientific world view by the earlier philosophers. The theory of Ideas, first formulated by Plato and then tidied up by Aristotle, is a result of this investigation. Another result is the Platonic-Aristotelian theory of science, with Aristotle's methodology of the deductive sciences as its most mature part. A third result is formal logic, towards which Plato's theory of Ideas and his dialectics were evolving, and to which Aristotle gave an exact, although fragmentary, formulation. A fourth result, which will be discussed in this chapter, is the discovery of the problems of conceptual analysis.

The questions: "What is justice?"; "What is meant by 'justice'?"; "What should we mean by 'justice'?" are of a kind that I shall call concept analytical. Any word—"democracy", "mind", "life", "time", "space", "number", "infinity", etc.—can give rise to exactly similar questions. These queries are clearly no more difficult to frame than the child's "Why?", and in themselves they are also about as indefinite as this. They do not, as they stand, demand a definite kind of answer. Nevertheless, Socrates, Plato, and Aristotle must be credited with being the first who interested themselves in systematically asking and trying to answer problems of this type. Any enquiry must in its very beginning take its rise from vague questions. If the vague question is fruitful and asked at the right time, it can stimulate intellectual effort, which with time permits us to replace that question by a family of more definite questions—and perhaps to give the relevant answers, too. I shall not attempt to prove that the framing of concept-analytical questions can be fruitful; practically the entire history of philosophy and science are evidence of this fact.

According to unanimous ancient testimonies, Socrates was the true discoverer of the problems of concept analysis. As he posed them, the questions were essentially critical. He who cannot explain what justice, for example, is—how can he pronounce opinions at all as to what behaviour is just and what is unjust? (How irritating this critique was for those whom Socrates interrogated is shown by the death sentence which was finally passed on him—although, of course, it had other causes as well.) In Socrates, as well as in his two great successors, however, the analysis of concepts was actually a multi-dimensional project as regards its motivation and its purpose. The critical intention was always there, it is true, but it was soon concealed by other motives inspired by metaphysical speculation. In what follows I have tried to disentangle the motives which, I think, can be discerned, and the result is a list of no less than seven rather disparate ones (nos. I–VII).

Generally speaking, the concept-analytical question as put by Socrates and his successors requires a definition for an answer. Socrates himself can hardly have developed an explicit theory of definition, even though his analytical practice points towards a theory. Plato and, even more so, Aristotle tried to work out a methodology of definitions.

The development of concept analysis in the sequence of thinkers Socrates—Plato—Aristotle is in many ways a confusing story. Progress and retrogression were interspersed; whereas critical judgement sharpened in one direction, fanciful speculation took over in another. When we consider the level from which these thinkers began, however, their shortcomings appear all too natural and their hard-won insights emerge in an even more admirable light.

25. THE SOCRATIC ANALYSIS OF CONCEPTS

Many reasons lend probability to the supposition that Plato's earliest dialogues reflect fairly faithfully what Socrates thought and said, or at least very well could have thought and said. It is also likely that, as the years passed, the Socrates of the dialogues came to have less and less similarity with the real man and that in the end Plato put his own views into the mouth of his teacher, views which had actually been quite foreign to him. The analysis of concepts in the later dialogues exhibits many features that distinguish it from the analysis in the earlier dialogues. By the "Socratic" analysis of concepts I here understand the kind of analysis that is found in the early dialogues, which I suppose to be genuinely Socratic.

As an analyst of concepts, Socrates seems to have been almost exclusively interested in exploring the significance of terms that either have a direct evaluative character— "good", "evil", "beautiful", "ugly", etc.—or denote traits of human character or patterns of behaviour especially relevant to ethical judgements: "friendship", "piety", "temperance", "courage", etc. The Socratic question which sets off the attempt at definition in the Platonic dialogues generally has the form: "What is friendship?", "What is piety?", and so on. The dialogues use no one standard wording for the "definitions" given as answers. A definition of friendship may be stated by the words "Friendship is . . .", or "he is a friend who . . .", or in yet some other fashion.

A. *The motives*

Why is Socrates—and/or Plato, the stage-manager of the literary Socrates figure—so interested in the search for definitions? The interest was fed above all, I believe, by three motives. In his *Memorabilia* Xenophon writes:

For he [Socrates] thought that those who knew the nature [definition] of things severally, would be able to explain them to others; but as to those who did not know, he said that it was not surprising that they fell into error themselves, and led others into it. He therefore never ceased to reason with his associates about the nature of things.[1]

Xenophon here points out:

Motive I: He who is in possession of a good definition of "*X*" —a good answer to the question: "What is *X*?"—is less exposed to mistakes when enquiring about *X* than he who does not possess it.

---

[1] Xenophon, *Memorabilia*, IV vi 1.

This is no doubt, on the whole, correct. At times, however, Socrates—or was it Plato?—seems to have pushed this correct idea to the point of absurdity. In the *Meno*, which will be discussed in detail presently, Socrates declines to discuss whether virtue can be taught or not because he does not yet know "what virtue is", i.e. the definition of virtue. In the *Lysis*, he even finds it strange that a person can consider himself a friend of someone although he does not know the definition of friendship. At such moments Socrates gives the impression of thinking that nothing at all can be known about X until the definition of X has been established. At times Socrates seems to lean also towards the opposite extreme. Not only does he underestimate the possibility of gaining knowledge about X without a previous definition, but he also overestimates the power bestowed by the definition. The definition sometimes becomes for him something of an "Open Sesame!" to the treasury of knowledge.

Socrates spent his life in discussion with the citizens of Athens. To make discussion, and in general, communication with others as fruitful as possible became a vital interest to him. In Xenophon's words quoted above, the following motive behind concept analysis comes to light.

Motive II: To frame definitions of the terms we use is an important means of making discussion fruitful.

The strength of this motive must grow the more we become aware of the possibility that the same word can mean different things to different people. In Aristotle, who was incomparably more alive to this than Socrates or Plato, motive II is far more prominent than it was in them.

Socrates' concept analysis was particularly concerned with ethically relevant terms. Assume that the correct definition of "the good" is "the good is pleasure". Assuming that we ought to strive for the good, this definition gives us the rule that we ought to strive for pleasure. The Socratic concept analysis springs also from:

Motive III: A correct definition of an ethical term can help us to find the morally right way, whereas an incorrect definition may lead us astray.

B. *The definitions of virtue in the dialogue* Meno

In order to discover what Socrates expected of a definition we must consider the definitions that are proposed for discussion in the early dialogues and the arguments advanced for and against them. The dialogue *Meno* probably does not, it is true, belong to Plato's Socratic period, but the discussion of virtue it contains seems nevertheless to be a good example of Socratic analysis. We shall now study it in some detail.

Socrates and Meno are the parties to the debate. The latter suggests one definition of virtue (or perhaps: civic ability) after another, but each time Socrates' critique forces him to withdraw it. The upshot of the discussion is merely that the two agree that the definitions suggested are unsatisfactory. I shall now present the definitions in order, together with Socrates' objections to them. For the sake of brevity, the arguments will be somewhat formalized.

Meno first suggests a series of partial definitions:

(I 1) If x is a man, then x is virtuous if and only if x is adept in managing the affairs of the state, thereby aiding his friends and confounding his enemies, etc.

(I 2) If x is a woman, then x is virtuous if and only if x takes good care of her house and is obedient to her husband.

(I 3) If x is a boy, then . . .

(I 4) If x is a girl, then . . .

and so on . . .

Socrates objects that what he wants is a single definition, not a whole series of them. More precisely, he claims that the statement "x is virtuous" must be supposed to have the same significance regardless of whether x is a man or a woman, a boy or a girl, etc.

Meno then suggests:

(II) x is virtuous if and only if x has the ability to rule over others.

This time Socrates' objection is to the effect that (II) is, as we would say today, both too narrow and too broad. It is too narrow because there are virtuous people—for example, virtuous slaves and virtuous boys—who have no ability to rule. It is too broad because not all who have the ability to rule are virtuous—for instance those who rule but not with justice.

Meno now proposes:

(III) x is virtuous if and only if
    (i) x desires the good, and
    (ii) x has the ability to attain the good.

Socrates does not claim that (III) is incorrect, but he is of the opinion that it can be simplified. Appealing to his doctrine that no one ever desires anything but what he believes to be good, and interpreting the statement "x desires the good" as "x desires what x believes to be good", he asserts that everyone desires the good. Condition (i) of (III) therefore states nothing that separates the virtuous from the non-virtuous, and it may be omitted.

In the light of Socrates' theory as to what man desires, definition (III) is thus seen to be equivalent to:

(IV) x is virtuous if and only if x has the ability to attain the good.

Socrates next asks Meno what he understands by "the good". Meno replies that he thinks of health, wealth, and so on.

Socrates and Meno now agree to replace (IV) by:

(V) x is virtuous if and only if x has the ability to attain health, wealth, and so on.

Does it make no difference, Socrates enquires, whether a man has the power to attain these things in a just or in an unjust manner?

Meno is thereby moved to make his final attempt at a definition:

(VI) x is virtuous if and only if x has the ability to attain health, wealth, and so on "with justice, or temperance, or piety, or some other kind (part) of virtue".

Socrates points out that this is what in modern terminology one would call a circular definition: to understand from (VI) what it means to be virtuous, one must know in advance what virtue is. With this, Socrates' and Meno's attempt to answer the question "What is virtue?" comes to an end.

C. *The nature of the Socratic definition*

The discussion between Socrates and Meno is interesting from several points of view. The various conceptions of virtue which are played out against each other give an insight into the plurality of moral views coexisting in Greece at the time. According to the first definition, virtue consists in properly fulfilling one's assigned role in the stratified society. The second definition emphasizes the special virtue of the aristocratic élite, and so on. In comparison with the previous definitions, the sixth and last seems a step towards a somewhat more individualistic and also more internalized notion of virtue. Here, however, I shall consider the discussion merely from a logical point of view. What logical properties did Socrates require of a definition?

(1) Obviously, Socrates and Meno are not trying to assign some suitable meaning to an expression whose established meaning they feel free to change. They investigate "what virtue is", in the same spirit in which the astronomer scans the movements of the planets. They want to find out what virtue is, or what it is that makes a person virtuous.

(2) Socrates' objection to (I) shows that he considers the word "virtuous" to have the same meaning regardless of the kind of person the word is applied to. He rejects Meno's not unreasonable idea that the expression has different meanings depending on whether the person is a man or a woman, a boy or a girl, and so on. Socrates thus rather dogmatically assumes the unambiguity of the term that is to be defined.

Plato can hardly have been blind to the fact that the same expression may have different meanings in different contexts or when used by different speakers. The very fact that he lets Meno put forward the first definition would seem to show this. How then could he hold on to assumptions (1) and (2)? Philosophers of modern times who have engaged in concept analysis in an essentially Socratic–Platonic spirit have often spoken of the "proper" or "correct" meaning of an expression. This "proper" meaning, they assume, is a unique thing existing beside the many improper meanings. Although Plato never stated anything quite like that, the assumption of unambiguous, proper meanings is tacitly made in the Socratic–Platonic concept analysis.

(3) From Socrates' objection to (II) it appears that exactly the same persons should fall under the term to be defined and the expression used for defining it. In modern terminology, a definition that Socrates would find acceptable must satisfy the requirement that the definiens and the definiendum have the same extension.

(4) Socrates' reduction of (III) to (IV) implies the requirement that the definiens should not contain any superfluous characteristics.

(5) Finally, Socrates' objection to (VI) shows that he requires a definition to be in some sense non-circular: the definiendum must not be presumed to be known in the definiens.

Would Socrates (or Plato) have been prepared to accept any (non-trivial) statement, "*A* is *B*", or (with a modern formalization), "*x* is *A* if and only if *x* is *B*", fulfilling the three requirements (3)–(5), as a correct definition of "*A*"? These seem to be the requirements mainly appealed to by Socrates in his critical discussion of definitions in Plato's early dialogues. Even in these dialogues, however, signs may at times be detected of the more rigorous demand that a definition should render the very idea, the essence, or form, for which the definiendum stands. Aristotle was later to supply a more precise formulation of this requirement through his doctrine of the predicables.

26. CONCEPTUAL ANALYSIS IN THE SHADOW OF THE THEORY OF IDEAS

A. *Definitions and the soul's communion with the Ideas*

The theory of Ideas created a new motive for the search of definitions:

Motive IV: To define a term that can be predicated of several particular things is a stage in the soul's communion with the Ideas.

In the *Seventh Letter* (supposing its authenticity), Plato says that there are three necessary prerequisites to our understanding of the Idea of the Circle, viz. first the designation "circle", secondly the definition of "circle" (that whose extremes are everywhere equidistant from its centre), and third the image of a circle (as drawn on a slate, for instance). When Plato speaks of the definition here, he seems to have in mind the verbal formulation of it. It consists, he says, of "verb and substantive". Although it is distinct from the knowledge of the Idea of the Circle, which is "in the soul", it is a necessary condition for the acquisition of this knowledge.

B. *Definitions and the order of nature*

In his later dialogues, Plato repeatedly expresses certain views on classification. A set of things can, of course, be classified in numerous ways. Human beings may, for example, be classified according to age, or colour of skin, or speech, etc. Whatever classification is selected in a given context should depend, we are accustomed to think today, upon the purpose for which the classification is to be employed. Plato, however, assumed that there is a correct classification of things that nature itself prescribes, so to speak. To classify persons as male and/or female is correct, to classify them as Greeks and/or barbarians is incorrect; to classify numbers as odd and even is correct, to classify them as those up to 1,000 and those above 1,000 is incorrect. The correct classification is determined by the Ideas: things constitute a natural class when they all partake of a common Idea.

The correct Platonic classification is a hierarchical system of the form shown in diagram (K). x, y . . . are here the individual objects to be classified. a and b are the two species under the genus A. A and B in turn are subdivisions of a higher family, and so on. As the diagram indicates, Plato supposed that the several species of a given genus are normally obtained by dichotomy. From the individuals we can proceed upwards in the hierarchy, level by level, until a highest category has been reached. Occasionally Plato seems inclined to assume that there is a single highest category. In the *Republic* he appears to put the Idea of the Good at the

(K)

Highest genus	α		
Genera	A	B	
Species	a	b	
Particulars	x, y....		

top of the hierarchy of Ideas, but in his later Pythagorean phase he was apparently inclined to give this position to the Idea of the One. (In the *Sophist* existence, sameness, and difference are considered as, in some sense or other, "the greatest kinds".)

On the basis of this theory of classification, Plato advanced a programme of definition. If a species is to be defined, we should start with some superior genus and then proceed downwards in the hierarchy, step by step, until the species is reached. In the *Sophist* he illustrates this procedure with an explanation, no doubt intentionally comical, of the art of angling (diagram (L)). It is not clear exactly what definition of the art of angling this division implies. It is obvious, however, that the definition should assign to the definiendum its proper place in a hierarchical system of classification. We can therefore register:

Motive V: To define is a step in the attempt to determine

Art	(L)
Creative	Acquisitive
By exchange	Coercive
Fighting	Hunting
Inanimate things	Living things
Land animals	Sea creatures
Waterfowl	Fish
By enclosure	By blows
By night	In daytime
Harpooning	*Angling*

the position of the definiendum in the natural hierarchy of genera and species.

C. *Definitions and the origin of things*

In his old age Plato's philosophy took on more and more of a mathematical and Pythagorean character. According to a report, he once announced a lecture at the Academy on the subject of "the Good". Many interested people came to hear him, but most of them left in disappointment since what he said seemed to them to be pure mathematics. Typical of this last phase of Plato's thought is what I shall call a quasi-genetic outlook as regard the analysis of concepts.

An example of this is provided by Plato's theory of the origin of the so-called ideal numbers from the One and the Indefinite Duality. The content of this theory is largely concealed in the obscurity of Pythagorean mysticism and our latter-day ignorance. The theory involves some method of generating the integers 1, 2 . . . Philologists, philosophers, and mathematicians have proposed many reconstructions of it. For my present purpose it is fortunately unnecessary to try to decide which of them is correct. Although it may not be the most plausible historically, let us pick out the simple interpretation suggested by the German mathematician Kurt Reidemeister.[2] According to him, the Platonic construction is based on the two operations:

$$\sigma x = 2x$$
$$\tau x = 2x + 1.$$

We then obtain the following series of definitions:

$$2 = \sigma 1$$
$$3 = \tau 1$$
$$4 = \sigma\sigma 1$$
and so on.

From an arithmetical point of view these definitions have little merit. What is noteworthy is that, according to Plato, the process of definition illustrates the "origin" or "genesis" of the ideal numbers. He seems to have thought that the

[2] K. Reidemeister, *Das exakte Denken der Griechen* (Hamburg: Classen & Goverts, 1949), pp. 35–6.

process of generation witnessed here somehow continues beyond arithmetic, and produces, not only the entire world of Ideas, but also the abstract figures considered in pure geometry.

This outlook is quasi-genetic since the generating process does not take place in time and is therefore imbued with an intense ambiguity. It both is and is not a matter of something being generated in the literal sense of the word. For those who share this outlook, the analysis of concepts acquires still another motive:

Motive VI: To define is a means of tracing the (non-temporal) genesis of things.

27. ARISTOTLE AS AN ANALYST OF CONCEPTS

No brief survey can do justice to the many perceptive analyses of concepts that fill so many pages of Aristotle's works and constitute one of his most important contributions to philosophy. Only a very general characterization will be given here.

Aristotle treats most of the concepts that were of importance to the scientific and philosophical discussion among the Greeks in his day. The basic concepts of logic, mathematics, linguistics, physics, ethics, and metaphysics were all reviewed and submitted to very thorough analysis in his writings. The Socratic–Platonic concept analysis was founded on the assumption that words have a proper, unambiguous meaning. Aristotle is in principle free of this *naïveté*. His analyses are usually introduced with the explanation that such and such a word can be used in such and such different meanings, and he then considers each of these in turn. In doing so he carries out a programme formulated in the *Topics*:

It is expedient to have investigated the number of meanings of a term, both in the interest of clarity (since a person knows what he is talking about better when he is aware of how many meanings it can have) and in order to ascertain that our reasoning agrees with the facts and is not mere word splitting. Because as long as it is not clear in how many ways a term is used, it is conceivable that he who enquires and he who replies do not have the same thing in mind . . . It helps us to avoid misleading and being misled . . .[3]

[3] Aristotle, *Topics*, I 18, 108ᵃ 18 ff.

In the same work Aristotle draws up a number of rules (seventeen) which are intended to help those who wish to find out "if a term has a number of distinct meanings or only one." Moreover, he stresses that we should not be satisfied merely with stating that a term has different meanings in different contexts, but must also try to explain each one of them.

For example, we should not rest with saying that fairness and courage are called "good" in one meaning and that that which contributes to strength and health is called so in another meaning, but we must also explain that the former are so called because of a certain inherent quality which they themselves possess, the latter because they lead to a certain result and not by virtue of some inherent quality.[4]

If Aristotle were to take part in a discussion between today's analytically and semantically oriented philosophers, he would not appear to be behind the times—perhaps rather the opposite.

28. ARISTOTLE'S THEORY OF DEFINITION

In the *Posterior Analytics* and in the *Topics* Aristotle presents at length a methodology of definition. It has very little in common with the methods he applied in his many analyses of concepts. Fortunately so, it is tempting to add. The methods he practised are far superior to the methodology he preached, which was strongly influenced by Plato's later philosophy.

A. *Definitions and the order of nature*

In Aristotle's, as in the elderly Plato's view, the theory of definition is closely tied up with the notion of a classification prescribed by nature. As in Plato, the natural classes are ordered hierarchically by a genus–species relationship, whose significance is not explained but taken for granted. A given class may have certain subclasses which are its immediate species and for which it is the immediate genus (Lat. *genus proximum*). Such a subclass may in turn be the immediate genus of further subclasses which are its immediate species, and so on. At the bottom of the hierarchy are the individual "substances". Next above them come the lowest species.

---

[4] Aristotle, *Topics*, I 15, 106ᵃ 4 ff.

The classes occupying any particular level of the hierarchy together constitute an exclusive and exhaustive classification of the substances, i.e. each substance belongs to exactly one such class. In the hierarchy the path from any substance to its highest genus runs through a finite number of intermediate levels. The hierarchy has thus the same form as in Plato with two exceptions: according to Aristotle, there are several highest genera, and he rejects the view that the immediate species of a genus are always formed by dichotomy.

Each species has what Aristotle calls its differentiating characteristic (Lat. *differentia specifica*) and this is uniquely determined by the species. The genus Animal has among its subclasses the species Man. It is, of course, easy to name a long list of characteristics that distinguish Man from the other members of the genus Animal. According to Aristotle, however, only one of these characteristics is the *differentia specifica*. In the case of Man he says that it is rationality. The relation between a species and its *differentia specifica* is as basic to his scheme as the genus–species relation, and it is left just as unexplained.

The *genus proximum* and the *differentia specifica* constitute the "essence" (Greek: *ousia*) of a species. To define a species is to indicate its essence and, hence, to name its *genus proximum* and its *differentia specifica*. The definition of Man, for example:

Man = Animal (*genus proximum*) which is rational (*differentia specifica*).

When Aristotle's theory of definition is combined with his doctrine of the natural hierarchy of classes, a series of consequences ensue which Aristotle himself stated. Some of them are:

(a) Only species are definable—thus, not individual substances, or *summa genera*, or *differentia specifica*.

(b) A definable entity has essentially only one definition, namely the definition by its *genus proximum* and its *differentia specifica*.

Let us mean by a "chain of definitions" a sequence D_1, D_2, D_3 . . . , where D_{j+1} is a definition of the genus which occurs in the definiens of D_j. Using this terminology, we can also derive the corollary:

(c) There exist no infinite chains of definitions.

If there were an infinite chain of definitions, the natural hierarchy of classes would have to contain an infinite sequence of levels, and such is not the case.

Thus far Aristotle's theory of definitions is essentially nothing but a development and sharpening of Plato's view that definitions are a means of tracing the order of nature.

B. *Definitions and the search for the logically simple*

Aristotle considers the essence of a species to be logically composed of its *genus* and its *differentia specifica*; the latter are two disjoint components of its essence. In this sense a species is never logically simple: it has at least two components. Further, since the *differentia specifica* is a component of the species but not of the genus, a genus is always something logically more simple than any of its species. This view entails the following assumptions:

(a) To define is to distinguish components in a logically compound essence.

(b) A chain of definitions in the sense just explained leads to progressively simpler essences.

(c) Simple essences cannot be defined.

These notions, which have their roots in the Platonic theory of Ideas and may be called "the microscope theory of definition", have been an important element in the philosophies of thinkers such as Descartes, Leibniz, Locke, Hume, Bolzano, and, in recent times, Russell. For all these thinkers, as for Aristotle, their interest in the analysis of concepts was sustained by:

Motive VII: To define is a means toward arriving at the logically simple components of reality.

C. *The doctrine of the predicables*

On the basis of his theory of classification and definition, Aristotle distinguished four relationships between a given species A and a property B so chosen that all A are B. According to Aristotle, four different cases can arise:

(i)   All *B* are *A*, and *B* constitutes *A*'s essence.
In this case *B* is said to be the "definition" of *A*.

(ii)   All *B* are *A*, but *B* does not constitute *A*'s essence.
In this case *B* is said to be a "property" of *A*.

(iii)   Some *B* are not *A*, but *B* is a component of *A*'s essence.
In this case *B* is either a genus under which *A* is directly or indirectly subsumed or the *differentia specifica* of *A* or of such a genus.

(iv)   Some *B* are not *A*, and *B* is not a component of *A*'s essence.
In this case *B* is said to be an "accidental" attribute of *A*.

We have an example of (i) in the definition of Man mentioned above, putting *A* = Man and *B* = Rational animal. An example of (ii) is obtained by making *A* = Man and *B* = Being that can laugh. An example of (iii) is obtained if we choose *A* = Man, *B* = Animal, or *B* = Rational. Taking *A* = Man and *B* = Featherless, we presumably get an example of (iv).

Of an acceptable definition one may require any one of a number of relationships between its definiendum and its definiens. The Socrates of Plato's early dialogues emphasized almost exclusively the demand for identity of extension. Aristotle's distinction between cases (i) and (ii) shows that he required something more. If *B* is a property of *A*, then *B* has the same extension as *A*, but nevertheless it cannot serve as a definition of *A*.

Aristotle's theory of the predicables is primarily concerned with the relations between a general concept *A*, belonging to the natural hierarchy of genera and species, and some other concept *B* such that all *A* are *B*. He also applies the theory, however, to the relations between individual substances and general concepts. If the natural class *A* bears one of the relations (i)–(iv) to *B* (e.g. *B* is a property of *A*), and if an individual substance belongs to *A*, Aristotle sometimes ascribes to the substance that same relation to *B* (e.g. *B* is said to be a property of the substance). This extension of the terminology is unfortunate, since by its means one can obviously arrive at contradictory results.

V

Ancient Logic

29. INTRODUCTION

A theoretical study of the principles of reasoning does not readily take place save in an environment where fairly complex logical reasoning is common. The thinking of the early natural philosophers may be described as conjecture and intuition stimulated by observation. The first eager dialecticians in Greek philosophy were the Eleatics, Parmenides and Zeno; the latter handled with virtuosity the method of proof called *reductio ad absurdum*. During the fifth century, in the time of the Greek Enlightenment, the Sophists ardently devoted themselves to proving and refuting all manner of theses, at times perhaps as an art for art's sake. In intellectual technique Socrates, and Plato also, were quite close to the Sophists. What immediately strikes a modern reader of Plato's works is how often he makes grave errors in arguments that presumably were intended to be rigorous. In Socrates' and Plato's time, the philosophers' love of argument does not seem to have been balanced by an equally well-developed feeling for logical accuracy. Such a setting appears to be ideal for the development of theoretical logic. It could be expected to commence as an attempt to raise the logical quality of discussion. Aristotle gives himself the credit of being the first theoretical logician. In his first works on logic, the *Topics* and *On Sophistical Refutations*, he gave rules of thumb on how to avoid logical blunders in a discussion and how to expose the errors of an opponent. Only gradually was logic transformed in Aristotle's hands from debating technique to the theoretical science that he developed in his logical masterpieces, the *Prior Analytics* and the *Posterior Analytics*.

Besides the philosophers, logical reasoning was practised especially by the mathematicians. In their field they quickly acquired much greater proficiency than did the philosophers in theirs. In his works on logic, Aristotle frequently takes his examples from mathematics. As far as its logical methods are concerned, Greek mathematics is unfortunately poorly charted territory. It is therefore now impossible to say to what extent the logician's rules of inference were abstracted from actual mathematical reasoning. So far as we know, the Greek mathematicians never evinced any interest in the problems of theoretical logic. In two respects, however, we may confidently assume an influence from mathematics upon logic: (a) The Platonic-Aristotelian ideal of science developed in close interaction with the rapidly advancing study of mathematics. This ideal envisages a deductive science in which theorems are deduced from axioms in a purely logical fashion. It must naturally have evoked the notion of a logic as an instrument to be used in passing from axioms to theorems. Aristotle seems to have considered his logic as just such an instrument, and his logical writings were to be collected later under the title of the *Organon* (the Instrument). (b) Mathematics probably also inspired the form in which Aristotle presented his most remarkable contribution to logic, the so-called syllogistic. Leibniz observed that here Aristotle was the first to think mathematically outside the traditional domains of mathematics.

One of the minor philosophical schools who considered Socrates as their spiritual father, the Megarics, developed a formal logic independently of Aristotle and along lines other than his. Whereas Aristotle's logic is best characterized as a class logic, the Megaric logic is a propositional logic. Diodorus Chronus and Philo of Megara (fourth century BC), were two of the foremost logicians of the Megaric school. Its ideas were taken up and developed by the Stoics. The leading Stoic logician seems to have been Chrysippus (third century BC). Logic was cultivated throughout ancient time, but the thinkers of late antiquity showed here as elsewhere a preference for obscure eclecticism, and they made few gains.

Aristotle is the only classical Greek logician whose writings on logic have been preserved. Not until the second century AD do we find another extant work in logic, by the physician Galen. There are several logical works by the commentators of late antiquity; often they are commentaries on Aristotle's *Organon.*

Inductive logic was relatively neglected. In a library in Herculaneum, however, a work by the Epicurean, Philodemus (first century BC), has been found which gives an account of the discussion on induction between the Epicureans, who favoured it, and the Stoics, who were somewhat obsessed by deduction.

None of the ancient philosophical schools seems to have attributed an independent value to the study of logic. Logic was an instrument, a weapon, a defence. Typical was the Stoic comparison of philosophy to an egg. Of the three parts of which they considered philosophy to consist, they likened logic to the protective shell, physics to the nutritive white, and ethics to the life-generating yolk. The Stoic moralist Epictetus (*c.* AD 100), rebukes the teachers of philosophy who ignore the problems of ethics for the study of logic and linguistic analysis. He caricatures a teacher as saying:

I promise you that I shall explain Chrysippus' doctrines for you as no one else can. I shall analyse his language and explain it completely. Perhaps I shall add a touch of Antipater's or Archidemos' subtlety.

To this Epictetus replies:

What! Is it for the sake of this that young men leave their native lands and parents—to come to listen to you explain linguistic trifles? Should they not instead return prepared to live and co-operate with others, calm and free from inner strife, provided with nourishment for the voyage of life, making it possible for them to meet whatever may come their way and thus distinguish themselves? And how can you offer them what you yourself are lacking in? Because from the very beginning your only activity has been analysing syllogisms . . .[1]

I am sure that more than one of the so-called analytical philosophers of our own time will have overheard a similar dialogue in his own mind.

One of Epictetus' thoughts on logic is independent of his interest in ethics:

Since it is reason that makes all other things articulate and complete, and reason itself must be analysed and made articulate, what is it that will effect this? Plainly, either reason itself or something else. That

[1] Epictetus, *Discourses*, III 21.

something else either is reason or will be something superior to reason, which is impossible. If it is reason, who again will analyse that reason? Because if it analyses itself, so can the reason with which we started. If we are going to call in something else, the process will be endless and unceasing.[2]

When Epictetus speaks of reason here, he obviously has in mind much the same thing as logical reasoning or logic. We may perhaps interpret his argument thus: When we take as the object of our study a logic L, can we then use L itself as the instrument of study, or do we have to resort to another logic, say L'? If the latter is the case, then in studying L' we ought to employ yet a third logic, say L'', and thus there arises an infinite regress, $L, L', L'' \ldots$ If, on the contrary, L' can be studied by means of L', then it should also be possible to study L by means of L. Epictetus' argument is in no way conclusive, but it is interesting in that it touches upon the modern distinction between logic and metalogic and upon all the problems that have come to light in this connection, but of which the Greek logicians were unaware.

Deductive Logic

30. ARISTOTLE'S SYLLOGISTIC

Swedish schoolboys of my generation learnt by heart the mnemonic verse, Barbara Celarent . . . , listing the syllogistic modes, and we were sometimes given as exercises syllogisms such as:

> No absent-minded person is an elephant.
> All professors are absent-minded.
> Hence, no professor is an elephant.

The Aristotelian syllogistic, on which school instruction unjustifiably cast an air of ridicule, will be described here in an abstract manner. In order to state Aristotle's ideas concisely, it will be useful to introduce some definitions—most of which are not in this form in his works.

By an Aristotelian term let us mean a general term that can be truly predicated of at least one object. The terms 'man', 'Greek', 'Athenian', are thus Aristotelian, whereas the terms

[2] Epictetus, *Discourses*, I 17.

'unicorn', 'four-sided circle', '2,000-year-old live mosquito' are not so. There does exist at least one man, at least one Greek, and so on, but there exists no unicorn, no four-sided circle, and so on. The Aristotelian syllogistic is a theory which concerns Aristotelian terms. An Aristotelian term may also be described as a term that represents a non-empty class, that is, a class that contains at least one member. The Aristotelian syllogistic is thus a theory of certain relationships between non-empty classes.

Aristotle intended the syllogistic to be a completely general theory. To achieve generality he introduced letters, today we would call them variables, for which we may mentally substitute any arbitrarily chosen Aristotelian terms. Let us here use the letters S, M, and P for this purpose and call them the term variables.

Aristotelian terms can function in statements of almost any structure. In the syllogistic, Aristotle takes into consideration only four types of simple statements, namely:

(A) All x are y
(B) No x are y
(C) Some x are y
(D) Some x are not y

where "some" may be interpreted as "at least one". For x and y, any of these term variables can be substituted. Let us call the formulas that result from such substitutions categorical formulas. The first variable, from the left, in a categorical formula shall be called the subject, and the second the predicate.

Now by a syllogism let us mean a formula that satisfies the following four conditions:

(i) It is of the form: If A and B, then C, where A, B, and C are categorical formulas;
(ii) A contains M and P;
(iii) B contains M and S;
(iv) C has S for its subject and P for its predicate.

Conditions (ii)–(iv) involve a number of symbolic conventions which are concerned with inessentials but greatly facilitate the analysis. Instead of the letters *S, M,* and *P,* we could, of course, have chosen any other letters or symbols whatsoever. Instead of subjecting *A* to condition (ii) and *B* to condition (iii), we could have done it the other way round. And so on. The basic idea behind the conventions is that we ignore the differences between such statements of type (i) as can be transformed into each other by a one-to-one exchange of term variables and/or by changing the order of the antecedent formulas *A* and *B*. From each set of formulas which can thus be transformed into each other, we pick out one formula to represent the set. We pick out just those formulas of type (i) that satisfy conditions (ii)–(iii), and we call them "the syllogisms", thereby ignoring all their many variants which can be obtained by the two operations just mentioned. An example of a syllogism is the so-called mode Barbara:

G 1. If all *M* are *P* and all *S* are *M*, then all *S* are *P*.

Let us further introduce the notion of a valid syllogism. A syllogism is valid if it becomes a true statement regardless of which Aristotelian terms are substituted for the variables. For example, if we insert the three Aristotelian terms, 'Greek', 'man', and 'Athenian', in the places of the letters *M, P,* and *S, G 1* is transformed into the assertion: 'If all Greeks are men and all Athenians are Greeks, then all Athenians are men.' This is a truth, though of a very trivial kind, and it is readily seen that *G 1* is turned into a similarly trivial truth no matter what Aristotelian terms we choose to substitute for the variables. *G 1* is therefore an example of a valid syllogism.

Aristotle's syllogisms have here been constructed as hypothetical statements of the form, 'If *A* and *B* then *C*'. However, Aristotle's words permit us with equal right to conceive of them as inference schemata of the form:

$$A$$
$$\frac{B}{\text{Hence, } C.}$$

An alternative reading of Barbara would thus be:

All *M* are *P*
All *S* are *M*

Hence, all *S* are *P*.

Aristotle set himself the problem of determining which syllogisms are valid and which are invalid. A simple combinatorial calculation shows that there are exactly 256 distinct syllogisms. Of these exactly twenty-four are valid. Of the valid syllogisms, Aristotle discusses fourteen in detail, explicitly states or indicates another five, and gives a mere hint concerning the existence of the remaining five. In a sense, thus, he completely solved the problem he had given himself.

Aristotle could have solved his problem by the simple but tedious method of going through all the 256 syllogisms, one by one, and deciding upon the validity of each. But his method was actually more elegant. *Inter alia* he proved the validity of the valid syllogisms by deducing them from *G 1* and:

G 2. If no *M* are *P* and all *S* are *M*, then no *S* are *P*.

Aristotle thus developed the system of valid syllogisms as an axiomatic theory, although his axiomatization does not satisfy the rigorous standards of logicians of today. As regards the invalid syllogisms, Aristotle developed methods whereby the invalidity of one syllogism can be derived from that of another and whereby entire classes of syllogisms can be simultaneously shown to be invalid. Aristotle's *Posterior Analytics*, in which he presents his syllogistic, is older than Euclid's *Elements*. It is therefore the oldest known axiomatic work.

Aristotle attributed great usefulness to his syllogistic. In his opinion, mathematical inferences are always made in accordance with some syllogism. In his theory of the nature of demonstrative science he even advances the opinion that the proper logical tools of such a science are the syllogisms of the first figure (where *M* is the subject of *A* and the predicate of *B*), being the scientifically most perfect. His appreciation of the syllogistic was exaggerated. In our time some people have been guilty of an opposite misjudgement when declaring it to be incorrect. What they usually have had in mind is that Aristotle's concept of valid syllogism refers exclusively to terms that can be truly predicated of at least one object. This limitation is unsuitable. We need a logic that can also be applied to terms that do not fulfil the Aristotelian condition, simply because we often do not know beforehand whether the terms we wish to use satisfy the condition or not. The limitation does not imply, however, that the Aristotelian syllogistic is incorrect within its own domain.

31. ARISTOTELIAN AND STOIC LOGIC

The syllogistic gives rise to an interesting problem. It is a deductive theory, and as such it requires a logical instrument for deducing its theorems from the basic assumptions. What logical instrument did Aristotle use in developing his syllogistic? He did not consider this matter systematically. *A priori* the following can be said about the necessary logical instrument. (a) An axiomatization of the syllogistic implies that we take certain syllogisms as postulates and deduce the remaining ones from them. The logical instrument used here must contain rules to the effect that, given certain syllogisms, we are justified in asserting certain others. We can compare the Aristotelian syllogisms to positions in a game of chess, and the deductive development of the syllogistic to the passage from one position to another. The rules just mentioned will then correspond to the rules of chess. (b) Aristotle's main interest in the syllogistic was concerned with the logical characteristics of such words as "all", "no", and "some". Along with these, however, such logically important words as "and" and "if—then" occur in Aristotelian syllogisms. The presupposed logical instrument must evidently furnish rules for operating with these words. They are used by Aristotle to construct compound statements from the simple ones. Thus they are *connectives* belonging to what is usually called the propositional (or sentential) logic.

Stoic logic is, in principle, just the kind of logical instrument the Aristotelian syllogistic requires. If we look upon an Aristotelian syllogism as an inference schema, we find that Stoic logic, in principle, offers us the proper tool for deriving such schemata from each other. Anticipating what is said in the next section, we may write the inference scheme Barbara in the form:

(i)   All M are P, All S are $M \rightarrow$ All S are P.

By Theorem 1 of Stoic logic, we may infer from (i):

(ii)   All M are P, Not: all S are $P \rightarrow$ Not: all S are M.

Replacing M by P and P by M, we rewrite (ii) as:

(iii)   All P are M, Not: all S are $M \rightarrow$ Not: all S are P.

If we apply the definition:

(iv)   Some x are not $y =$ Df   Not: all x are y,

(iii) becomes the syllogism Baroco (of the second figure):

(v)   All P are M, Some S are not $M \rightarrow$ Some S are not P.

32. THE STOIC LOGIC OF PROPOSITIONS

A basic concept of Stoic logic is the notion of a proposition (*axioma*). A proposition is defined by the Stoics as a "complete *lekton* (content of thought) which by itself asserts something". In addition to propositions, the complete *lekta* (concerning the concept of *lekton*, cf. §36) includes questions, commands, and requests; these differ from propositions precisely in that they do not of themselves assert anything. A proposition is always either true or false.

Propositions are either simple or compound. A compound proposition is one that contains two or more occurrences of other propositions. Some examples of compound propositions are: 'It is day, and the sun is shining', 'If it is day, then it is light', 'It is day, or it is night'. Such queer propositions as the following are also compound: 'It is day, and it is day', 'If it is day, then it is day', 'It is day, or it is day'. In compound propositions of this kind, only one simple proposition, 'it is day', occurs but it has two distinct occurrences, a first and a second, reading from left to right, and so the entire proposition is compound. A proposition that is not compound is simple. Examples of simple propositions are: 'It is day', 'All men are mortal', 'Someone is walking', 'It is not day'. In negative propositions such as the last-mentioned one, the Stoics preferred to prefix the word 'not' to what is negated, thus writing 'Not: it is day'. This artificial mode of expression has the merit of showing exactly what is being negated.

In order to be able to describe concisely the Stoic theory of inference, it is useful to introduce certain symbols which were not employed by the Stoics. The letters $A, B, C \ldots$ will be used to represent arbitrary propositions. (For the same purpose the Stoics themselves used expressions such as "the first", "the second", "the third", and so on.) By the formula '$A, B \ldots \rightarrow F$', we shall express the assertion that the conclusion F may be validly inferred from the premisses $A, B \ldots$ (The Stoics said '$A, B \ldots$; hence F'.) The notation: neg(A), shall be used with the following meaning: If A begins with the word 'not', then neg(A) is what remains when this word is omitted; if A does not begin with 'not', then neg(A) is the result of prefixing 'not' to A. (The Stoics spoke here of the "opposite" of A.)

The Stoics are reported to have laid down five basic rules of inference which in our notation run like this:

R 1. If A then $B, A \rightarrow B$

R 2. If A then $B,$ neg(B) $\rightarrow$ neg(A).

R 3. Not: A and $B, A \rightarrow$ neg(B)
Not: A and $B, B \rightarrow$ neg(A)

R 4. A or $B, A \rightarrow$ neg(B)
A or $B, B \rightarrow$ neg(A)

R 5. A or $B,$ neg(A) $\rightarrow B$
A or $B,$ neg(B) $\rightarrow A$

The Stoics are also said to have stated four so-called theorems, which they used to deduce further rules from the five basic ones. The first theorem was stated in the words: "If from two /say A, B/ a third /say C/ is inferred, one of the two /say A/ together with the opposite of the third /i.e. neg(C)/ yields the other."[3] In modern symbolism, part of this rule can be expressed by the inference schema:

---

[3] Cf. Bochenski, *Formale Logik* (Munich: Verlag Karl Alber Freiburg, 1956), 22.12.

(1)
$$\frac{A, B \to C}{A, \text{neg}(C) \to \text{neg}(B)}$$

where the horizontal line signifies that it is admissible to go from what stands above the line to what stands below. To get the full force of the first theorem, as quoted, we must understand theorem (1) in such a sense that the order of the premisses both above and below the line is inessential. Thus, the schema:

(2)
$$\frac{A, B \to C}{B, \text{neg}(C) \to (A)}$$

is also covered by the first theorem. The second theorem is not known. The third was stated in the words: "When from two /say *A, B*/ a third /say *C*/ is inferred and one of the two /say *A*/ can be syllogistically inferred from external /premisses, say *X*/, then the third /*C*/ can be inferred from the remaining /*B*/ and those external ones /*X*/".[4] In modern symbolism, part of this rule can be represented by the schema:

(3)
$$\frac{A, B \to C \qquad X \to A}{X, B \to C} \,,$$

where *X* represents some set of propositions.

To get the full force of the third theorem it must again be understood here that the order of the premisses is everywhere inessential. The fourth theorem has been lost.

There are some examples extant of how the Stoics used their theorems in demonstrating further rules. One of the rules they derived was:

R 6. If *A* then if *A* then *B*, *A* → *B*.

The following two propositions are instances of the first rule:

(1) If *A* then if *A* then, *B*, *A* → If *A* then *B*.
(2) If *A* then *B*, *A* → *B*.

If we now make use of the third theorem, we can infer from (1) and (2):

(3) If *A* then if *A* then *B*, *A*, *A* → *B*.

[4] Cf. ibid. 22.13.

If—as seems probable—the Stoics regarded the repetition of a premiss as an inessential feature of rule of inference, (3) is the same as *R 6*, which was to be proved. The Stoics are supposed to have similarly deduced "innumerably many" other rules.

Stoic logic, as the sources present it today, can be considered a fragment of a logical system of the type now called "Gentzen systems". One may ask whether the two lost theorems, the second and the fourth, could have been such that in its original form this logic was a complete Gentzen calculus for some propositional logic. It is, however, difficult to conceive any theorems to this effect. (A reconstruction suggested by Oskar Becker seems highly improbable.[5]) A serious warning against overestimating the ingenuity of the Stoics, or the purity of our sources, is the fact that *R 2* follows from *R 1* by Theorem 1 and is therefore a redundant postulate.

With an eye to the discussion in the next section, it is interesting to deduce some further rules of Stoic logic.

R 7. A, neg(*B*) → Not: if *A* then *B*
This rule follows directly from *R 1* by the first theorem.

R 8. A, B → *A* and *B*
This follows from *R 3* by the first theorem.

R 9. A, B → Not: *A* or *B*
This follows from *R 4* by the first theorem.

R 10. Neg(*A*), neg(*B*) → Not: *A* or *B*
This follows from *R 5* by the same theorem.

33. MEGARIC–STOIC DISCUSSION OF TRUTH CONDITIONS
FOR COMPOUND PROPOSITIONS

Stoic logic deals with the four propositional connectives: 'not', 'and', 'or', and 'if—then'. Obviously, what logical rules hold for these connectives depends upon how they are interpreted. If, for example, 'or' is interpreted in one way, certain logical rules are correct; if it is interpreted in another way, other rules turn out to be correct. The Megarics and the

---

[5] O. Becker, *Zwei Untersuchungen zur antiken Logik* (Wiesbaden, 1957).

Stoics held very explicit views as to the conditions under which statements of the types: '*A* and *B*', '*A* or *B*', 'If *A* then *B*' are true or false, and concerning the two latter types there were controversies.

For the negation, 'Not *A*', they do not seem to have laid down explicit truth conditions, but their usage corresponds to the following two conditions:

If *A* is true, then 'Not *A*' is false.
If *A* is false, then 'Not *A*' is true.

If we denote truth by $\bar{T}$ and falsity by *F*, these rules can be summarized by means of a table (M), now usually called a table of truth values (*T* and *F* being the two truth values considered), or a truth table.

(M)

A	Not *A*
T	*F*
F	*T*

For the conjunction, '*A* and *B*', the Stoics accepted the truth conditions as shown in table (N). The previously proven

(N)

A	*B*	*A* and *B*
T	*T*	*T*
F	*T*	*F*
T	*F*	*F*
F	*F*	*F*

rule *R 9* obviously corresponds to the first row of this table; both *R 9* and the first row indicate that if *A* as well as *B* are true, then '*A* and *B*' is also true.

If a truth table for the conditional 'If *A* then *B*' is to agree with principles of the Stoic propositional logic, it will clearly have to be set out as in table (O). The rule *R 8* which we deduced in the preceding section implies that if *A* is true and *B* false, then 'If *A* then *B*' is false also. But what truth values should we put in the empty spaces? Is it possible to set up a

(O)

A	B	If A then B
T	T	—
F	T	—
T	F	F
F	F	—

truth table for 'If A then B' at all? Different opinions on this matter were rife among the Megarics and Stoics. Philo of Megara thought that such a truth table could be established. More specifically, he wished to fill all the blank spaces with Ts, thus anticipating the modern concept of material implication. According to this interpretation the conditional 'If A then B' is true in all cases except when A is true but B false. Others, among them possibly Chrysippus, maintained that 'If A then B' is true only when the negation of B is inconsistent with A. This interpretation cannot be expressed in the form of a truth table. Those who favoured this interpretation anticipated the modern idea of strict implication. Diodorus Chronus held yet a third view. Sextus Empiricus gives an account of no less than four distinct interpretations of the conditional. The extant part of Stoic logic retains its validity whether the conditional is interpreted as material implication or as something stronger. The controversy among logicians on this point was perhaps mainly concerned with the interpretation of common usage. The lively interest that the Greek philosophers took in the meaning of conditional statements in the second century BC is attested by the poet Callimachus who said, in an epigram, that even the ravens on the roofs croaked about what conditionals are true.

To conform with the Stoic propositional logic, a possible truth table for the disjunction 'A or B' must have the entries as shown in table (P). Rules $R\ 10$ and $R\ 11$, which were

(P)

A	B	A or B
T	T	F
F	T	—
T	F	—
F	F	F

deduced above, tell us that '*A* or *B*' is false when both *A* and *B* are true and also when they are both false. What truth values should be put into the blank spaces in the table? Is it possible to set up a truth table for the disjunction at all? On this point, too, there existed different opinions among the Stoics. Some thought that '*A* or *B*' should be accepted as true whenever just one of *A* and *B* is true. Other Stoic logicians refused to accept the disjunction as true unless it is necessary that just one of them is true. This interpretation cannot be rendered by a truth table. Here again, Stoic propositional logic, as we know it today, is compatible with either interpretation, and here also the disagreement may have been concerned with the understanding of ordinary usage.

Semantics

34. ARISTOTLE ON LANGUAGE, MEANING, AND TRUTH

A. *The semantic trichotomy*

According to Aristotle, written words are symbols for spoken words, and spoken words in turn are symbols for thoughts. Thoughts, finally, are images of things. If we leave aside the distinction, of minor philosophical interest, between written and spoken words, we find that Aristotle introduces the trichotomy:

Word—symbol for—*Thought*—image of—*Thing*.

Like so many of the views that obtained their first extant explicit statement in Aristotle, this view has been one of the great themes of Western philosophical thought. In the seventeenth century, it formed one of the most basic assumptions of the philosophies of Descartes, Spinoza, Malebranche, Geulincx, Leibniz, and Locke. In Locke, it tended to degenerate into the dichotomy:

Word—symbol for—*Idea*,

a degeneration which was to have such an influence upon Berkeley and Hume.

B. *Statements and their truth values*

Thoughts are of two kinds: such as are either true or false, and such as are neither. An example of the first kind is the thought 'All men are white'. Examples of the second kind are its constituent ideas 'man' and 'white'. According to Aristotle thoughts of the first kind always involve a combination or separation of other thoughts. Presumably he would consider that in 'All men are white', the thought 'man' is combined with the thought 'white', whereas these thoughts are separated in 'No man is white'. Assertions, according to Aristotle, are such sentences as "have in them either truth or falsity", i.e. are either true or false. Prayers are mentioned as examples of sentences which are neither true nor false and, hence, are not assertions.

The words 'true' and 'false' have two fields of application in Aristotle. Certain thoughts, "discourses of the soul", are true or false, in one meaning of the words. In another meaning, certain linguistic expressions are true or false. The two usages are parallel: an expression is true (false) if and only if the thought expressed is true (false). The notions of truth and falsity are explained as follows:

To say of something that is, that it is not, or of what is not, that it is, is false; whereas to say of something that is, that it is, and of something that is not, that it is not, is true.[6]

From the context it is clear that this explanation was intended to have corollaries of the forms:

(i) If A, then to say 'not A' is false. (ii) If not A, then to say 'A' is false. (iii) If A, then to say 'A' is true. (iv) If not A, then to say 'not A' is true. We get the particular corollaries of the explanation by putting particular statements in the place of the letter A. An instance of (i) is, e.g., "If Socrates is mortal, then to say 'Socrates is not mortal' is false."

C. *Truth values of statements about the non-existent*

The Law of Contradiction and the Law of the Excluded Middle which Aristotle stated imply:

(a) Of any statement and its negation, one is true and the other false.

[6] Aristotle, *Metaphysics*, IV 7, 1011^b 26 ff.

In its general form (a) may appear intuitively evident, but it gives rise to difficulties when applied to certain expressions which seem to be legitimate statements. The statement "Apollo is not mortal" is the negation of the statement "Apollo is mortal". Now by (a), one of these is true and the other is false. But which is which? Using another example Aristotle decided that the statement "Apollo is not mortal", is true, and the statement "Apollo is mortal" is false. He seems inclined to generalize this decision to a rule of the following import:

> (b) If the subject S does not exist, then to affirm a predicate of S is false and to deny it is true.

The rule raises the question how to decide in a non-arbitrary way when a statement is positive and when negative. The occurrence of the word 'not', or of any other phrase with the same import, cannot be decisive, as is readily seen. Instead of saying "Apollo is not mortal", we could just as well say "Apollo is immortal". If the word 'not' makes a statement negative, then "Apollo is not immortal" ought to be true, by principle (b). This, however, says exactly the same thing as "Apollo is mortal", which according to the same principle should be judged to be false.

35. THE LAWS OF THOUGHT

A. *Aristotle on the laws of thought*

There exist, Aristotle maintains in the fourth book of the *Metaphysics*, certain basic principles which we must accept in order to be able to pursue the study of any science or take part in any rational discussion. One of these principles is the Law of Contradiction. Two Aristotelian formulations of this law are:

It is impossible for anything at the same time to be and not to be.

One side of a contradiction is false.

Another such principle is the Law of the Excluded Middle (in Latin: *tertium non datur*, 'there is no third'):

There cannot be an intermediate between contradictories.

One side of a contradiction must be true.[7]

---

[7] Ibid. IV 4, 1006^a 2; IV 8, 1012^b 12; IV 7, 1011^b 23; IV 8, 1012^b 10.

Aristotle discusses at length the difficulties that arise if these laws are rejected. But they cannot, on his view, be proven on the basis of any ulterior assumptions. He takes them to be basic principles of the science of "being as being", which he considered the most general and most fundamental of the sciences, and to which he gave the name of "first philosophy". (In modern times the two laws, together with certain other logical principles such as the so-called Law of Identity, have been brought together under the designation "laws of thought". As Frege and Husserl have shown, the designation can easily become misleading, and it is kept here merely as a heading.)

B. *The Law of the Excluded Middle and the future*

In Aristotle's work, *On Interpretation* (ch. 9), there occurs an interesting discussion which throws a certain doubt upon the universal validity of the Law of the Excluded Middle. Assume that someone says today:

A sea battle will take place tomorrow.

Let us use the letter p as a symbol for this proposition. Now according to the Law of the Excluded Middle,

I.   Either p or not-p.

In the discussion it is assumed that the following postulates hold:

IIa. If p, then it is necessary that p.

IIb. If not-p, then it is necessary that not-p.

If we combine I and II, we obtain the conclusion:

III.   Either it is necessary that p, or it is necessary that not-p.

But apparently the opposite of III holds for p:

IV.   It is possible that not-p, and it is also possible that p.

It can plausibly be said, "A sea battle may take place tomorrow, but also it may not take place tomorrow." If we accept II, III, and IV, then we must reject I, and hence also the Law of the Excluded Middle of which I is a corollary.

Three different views were put forward with regard to this argument. Aristotle's attitude toward the argument is somewhat unclear in the extant text of *On Interpretation*. He pointed out, however, that IIa (and analogously IIb) can be interpreted in two distinct ways:

(i) If p, then it is necessary that p.

(ii) It is necessary that if p, then p.

Whereas (i) is needed for the desired refutation of the Law of the Excluded Middle, only (ii) is an evident logical thesis. Aristotle seems thus to accept I and IV, but not II. A statement p about the future with the property that both p and not-p are possible was said by the medieval philosophers to represent a "future contingency" (*futurum contingens*). Aristotle appears to have considered the Law of the Excluded Middle as being logically consistent with the existence of future contingencies, and to have accepted both the law and the existence.

Despite Aristotle's telling criticism, it seems that both the Stoics and the Epicureans admitted II. In any event, they seem to have considered the Law of the Excluded Middle to be inconsistent with the existence of future contingencies. The Epicureans incorporated the theory of chance events and the freedom of the will (ultimately due to the random deviation of atoms from their given paths of motion) in their system. They considered these theories to imply the existence of future contingencies, which they also accepted, and they felt obliged to reject the Law of the Excluded Middle in its general form. The Stoics espoused the idea that everything that happens is predestined, and therefore they denied the existence of future contingencies. They saw no obstacle to accepting the Law of the Excluded Middle in its general form.

The debate on these questions continued into the Middle Ages, when each of the three views still had its sympathizers. When the Polish logician Łukasiewicz presented his many-valued logics (i.e. logics dealing with more truth values than just the two of truth and falsity) in 1920, he was inspired by this classical debate.

36. MEANING AND REFERENCE IN STOIC LOGIC

Plato's theory of Ideas contains an implicit distinction between what could be called the meaning of an expression and its reference. The word 'horse' stands for the Idea of Horse, but at the same time it also, in some sense, refers to all existing things that partake of that Idea, i.e. all horses. If we permit ourselves to call the Idea of Horse the "meaning" of the word and the existing horses its reference, something that Plato did not, we get the distinction with respect to the kind of words with which the theory of Ideas is concerned. In Aristotle's works, especially in the *Categories*, we also find hints of a distinction between meaning and reference. It was the Stoics, however, who were the first to develop a semantics which makes systematic use of such a distinction.

The Stoics distinguished between the linguistic expression, its meaning (the thought-content expressed, *to lekton*) and the existent things to which the expression refers. In their thinking about language, they thus apply the trichotomy:

Expression—Meaning—Reference

The generic name "man", for instance, has a meaning that is distinct from existing men. In order to comprehend this meaning we need only understand the English language, but in order to know men we must observe the world. The Stoics maintained a kind of materialism according to which material bodies are the only things there are. Accordingly they taught that all expressions refer only to material bodies. Their doctrine that meanings are incorporeal contributed to sharpening the distinction between meaning and reference, but also created a difficult metaphysical problem. If meanings are not bodies and only bodies exist, how then can words have meanings?

The Stoics also applied their trichotomy to expressions other than generic names. Their theory, so far as we know it, can be summarized in a diagram (Q). Although the details of this theory are obscure, it is interesting as the first attempt to create a systematic semantics and as a fore-runner of modern theories of the type that Bolzano, Frege, Church, Carnap, and many others, have developed.

Designation	Meaning	Reference
Proper name ("Socrates")	Uniquely characterizing property (perhaps that of being the main character in Plato's dialogues)	A particular thing (Socrates)
Generic name ("man")	Common property (the property of being a rational animal)	Several particular things (men)
Predicate ("drinks absinthe")	Property	
Statement *(logos)* ("It is night.")	Proposition *(axioma)* (the proposition that it is night)	

Selected Problems

37. LOGICAL PARADOXES

Logical paradoxes of the kind first proposed by the Megaric Eubulides were eagerly discussed by the Stoics. In the Middle Ages this kind of paradox became a fixed theme in the debates of the Scholastics, and in our own day some of them have acquired a new interest in the context of modern logic. The most substantial of these Stoic paradoxes are The Liar and the Electra. Also the paradox The Bald Man appears to have a surviving philosophical interest.

A. *The paradox of The Liar*

This paradox appeared in many different guises in antiquity. In its most complete form it runs like this. Assume that someone says, "I am now lying." Is he speaking the truth, or not? If his statement is true, then he is lying and thus it is false, and if his statement is false, then he is not lying and hence it is true. If we suppose that the statement is either true or false, then we are forced to conclude that it is both true and false. Let us set out the structure of the paradox in formal terms. Instead of the proposition, "I am now lying", we may use its equivalent, "What I am now saying is false". A first premise for the paradox is then:

(i) What I am now saying = "What I am now saying is false."

The other two premisses of the paradox are:

(ii) If the statement, "What I am now saying is false", is true, then what I am now saying is false.

(iii) If the statement, "What I am now saying is false", is false, then what I am now saying is not false.

If we postulate further:

(iv) Either what I am now saying is true, or what I am now saying is false,

then it follows:

(v) What I am now saying is both true and false.

Chrysippus is reported to have written several books on this paradox which constituted a stumbling-block for Stoic logic. A testimony to its fame in antiquity is the fact that St. Paul seems to allude to it in his letter to Titus 1: 12.

To common sense it might seem obvious that the statement, "What I am now saying is false", is devoid of sense if its subject phrase, "What I am now saying", is construed as referring to that very statement. That it is possible to arrive at a contradiction by using the operations of formal logic on a piece of nonsense does not strike us as being paradoxical. Unfortunately, there exist paradoxes closely related to The Liar, which cannot be ruled out on the same ground with equal plausibility. In our time, The Liar has been discussed especially by Bertrand Russell (whose theory of the orders of propositions was intended to supply a solution of it) and by Alfred Tarski (who refers the term "truth" to the semantics of the object language and requires the semantics to be formulated in a special metalanguage, whereby it becomes impossible to state the paradox). One of the most remarkable results in modern logic, Gödel's famous theorem on the existence of formally undecidable sentences, builds upon an idea that is akin to The Liar.

B. *The Electra paradox*

When he returned home, Orestes was not recognized by his sister, Electra. In this situation, the following two statements are both correct:

(1) Electra knows that Orestes is her brother.

(2) Electra does not know that the man before her is her brother.

But it is also true that:

(3) Orestes is identical with the man before her.

Thus Electra knows and yet does not know that one and the same man is her brother. This paradox seems to constitute a counter-example to the apparently evident logical thesis:

(4) If something holds of a and the same does not hold of b, then a and b are not identical.

In trying to solve this paradox, one may look for some reformulation of the premisses such that principle (4) becomes inapplicable to them, or for some limitation of this principle to the same effect. Exploring the first alternative, one could, e.g., restate (2) and (3) in accordance with Bertrand Russell's theory of descriptions:

(2¹) Electra does not know that there is exactly one man who stands before her and is her brother.

(3¹) There is exactly one man who stands before her and is identical with Orestes.

Another way out is indicated by the Stoic semantics: it might be assumed that Electra's knowledge concerns the *lekton* expressed by the sentence, "Orestes is my (Electra's) brother", and that her ignorance concerns the different *lekton* expressed by the sentence, "The man before me (Electra) is my (Electra's) brother". Accordingly, it might be assumed that the expressions, "Orestes" and "the man before her" represent their *lekta* rather than their references in (1) and (2). In (3), on the other hand, they stand for their references, not their *lekta*. It is not known that the Stoics proposed this solution, however. In the nineteenth century,

Frege suggested this method for the solution of similar logical puzzles. In trying the second of the two *a priori* possible methods of solution, one might look for reasons why the formulation (4) should be rejected as too general. Taking $F(a)$ to be some statement about a, we would thus abandon the idea that the non-identity of a and b can always be inferred from the truth of $F(a)$ and the falsity of $F(b)$. The inference is justified, we would have to maintain, only when the statement $F(a)$ is of a particular kind. This method of solving logical puzzles akin to "Electra" has been tried by Carnap and others in recent times.

C. *The paradox of Baldness*

One version of this paradox is as follows. The following seems a fairly plausible thesis:

(a) If a man with n strands of hair is bald, then one with $n + 1$ strands is also bald.

Since a man with no strand of hair is bald, then by (a) so is a man with 1 strand, one with 2 strands, etc. Continuing the argument we can show that any man is bald. (A similar argument occurs in Cicero. Using the principle:

(b) If n is a small number, then $n + 1$ is a small number,

he proves that all numbers are small.)

The conclusion to be drawn from the paradox of the Bald Man is clear; the principle (a) applies only to sufficiently small numbers n. But then when does it cease to apply? Here we have the kernel of the paradox. It is impossible to indicate just when the applicability ceases, or where the boundary between baldness and non-baldness lies. If we go through the series of possible cases:

F_n: The number of strands of hair on A's head is n
($n = 1, 2 \ldots$)

then we find that for some time in the cases $F_0, F_1, F_2 \ldots$, A must be considered as bald, that gradually there appears a stage when a classification is impossible, and that at last A must be classified as non-bald. If we apply the Law of the Excluded Middle on one of the intermediate cases F_n, we obtain the proposition:

Either *A* is bald or *A* is not bald.

If this is a truth, it appears that a closer study of the case F_n should lead to a decision between the alternatives: *A* is bald, *A* is not bald. But this is not so. A decision can be reached only after agreeing to change the use of the word "bald", i.e. by a more or less arbitrary precise formulation of its meaning. Such ambiguous terms as "bald" seem thus to be in conflict with the Law of the Excluded Middle. It may have been a feeling for this conflict that made the ancient philosophers take such an interest in the Bald Man.

The problem which the ancient logicians may have sensed can be restated as follows. Are we entitled to incorporate, in a language containing vague terms, a formal logic which includes the Law of the Excluded Middle in its general form? Since vague terms occur in all regions of speech, with the possible exception of pure logic and mathematics, and as the Law of the Excluded Middle appears a fundamental principle to our logical intuition, the problem is clearly one of major interest. Perhaps the question can be answered in this way: we are justified in doing so, but when we do it we anticipate a precise formulation of the terms of our language which has not yet been, and most probably never will be, carried out.

38. THE THEORY OF INDUCTION

Those ancient schools of philosophy which, like the Pythagoreans, Plato, and Aristotle, modelled their scientific ideal on the pattern of mathematics, generally had a low regard for the scientific value of induction, and on the whole they neglected the study of its theory. Induction was, of course, used in the natural sciences during antiquity, and in several disciplines, above all in medicine, an inductive research programme was devised in conscious opposition to the mathematically inspired epistemologies. On the philosophical level, the inductive method had its most ardent defenders among the Epicureans, whereas the Stoics and Sceptics were on the whole critical of it. The Epicurean Philodemus (first century BC) wrote a work *On the Methods of Proof*, which is preserved in parts and which today is our most detailed source of knowledge of the Stoic–Epicurean controversy.

The Stoics and Epicureans seem to have been in agreement on classifying all things as follows:

1. Things that are immediately perceived, or are evident. For the knowledge of these things no inference, deductive or inductive, is necessary.

2. Things that are not immediately perceived, or are non-evident. These things can in turn be divided into the following three subclasses:

2a. Things that, because of their nature and the limitations of our understanding, will for ever remain unknown. The question whether the number of the stars is odd or even would come under this class.

2b. Things that are not perceived here and now, but could be perceived, in some other place, or at some other time.

2c. Things that because of their nature can never be perceived, but nevertheless can be known to us. According to the Epicureans, the atoms and the void belong to this category.

The Epicureans believed that inference by analogy, or induction, enables us to gain knowledge of phenomena in 2b and 2c. Some examples of analogies mentioned by Philodemos are: (i) Since Plato is a man, we can infer that Socrates is a man. Since Epicurus is a man, we can infer that Metrodorus is a man. The inferences Philodemus has in mind here, can, I think, be spelled out more completely as follows: from (a) the innumerable known similarities between Plato and Socrates (save the fact that Socrates, too, is a man), and (b) the fact that Plato is a man, we are entitled to infer by analogy that (c) Socrates is a man. The arguments of this type conform to the pattern:

$$\frac{a \text{ is } Q}{b \text{ is } Q},$$

where a and b are known to be similar things. If the similarity is P, and its existence is raised to an explicit premiss, the pattern becomes the more familiar,

$$\frac{a \text{ is } P \text{ and } Q}{b \text{ is } P}$$
$$\overline{b \text{ is } Q}$$

(ii) From the fact that all men in our experience are mortal, we can proceed by analogy to the conclusion that all men, unobserved as well as observed, are mortal. The pattern of this second argument is:

$$\frac{\text{All observed } P \text{ are } Q}{\text{All } P \text{ are } Q}$$

In both cases, the Epicureans applied the word "analogy" to the similarity P as well as to the entire inference. Philodemos stressed that the similarity, on which an analogical inference is based, ought to be a strong one, and that, in inferences of type (ii), our observations must have covered a rich enough sample of Ps.

The Stoic criticisms of the Epicurean doctrine of analogy hit at many distinct aspects both of the general doctrine and of its particular applications by the Epicureans. The fundamental point of the critique was that inferences by analogy lack the "necessity" of deductive inferences and, hence, cannot be relied upon. The same objection was to be repeated by the Sceptics of late antiquity and by the British empiricists in the seventeenth and eighteenth centuries. The Epicureans granted that analogy has no necessity, but they maintained that analogy may have a force which makes it "inconceivable" that its premisses be true but its conclusion false. This "inconceivability" was enough for them.

VI

The Art of Living: Morals and Salvation

39. NATURE AND CONVENTION: THE SOPHISTS

In the fifth century BC, there appeared in the Greek world a kind of teacher of practical wisdom, the Sophist, who went from city to city, and, in return for a fee, gave instruction on how best to manage one's personal affairs and those of the state. Perhaps some of them deserved the contempt which Plato so often showed them, but many seem to have been seriously interested in moral and political problems. One of the questions they discussed was whether the rules that hold in society have a basis in nature (*physis*) or are merely a matter of convention (*nomos*). Different Sophists gave different answers. Whereas some held a conservative view, most of them seem to have levelled, in the name of "nature", a radical critique against the prevailing order. According to one Sophist trend of thought, all men are by nature free and equal, and the first socialists are found among the sponsors to this view. Some Sophists maintained that nature countenances only the right of the stronger. The most famous Sophist of all, Protagoras (*c.*481–411 BC)—who, like several other philosophers in Athens, incurred the accusation of impiety and escaped sharing the fate of Socrates only by flight—defended the thesis that "man is the measure of all things". Apparently he meant that something *is* such and such for a person whenever it *appears* to him to be such and such. He had in mind both sense perception and moral judgement.

The Sophist distinction between nature and convention was taken up by later schools of ancient philosophy, especially by the Stoics. By way of the medieval ideas about the law of nature it passed on the natural-law philosophy which played such an important part in jurisprudence and political theory during the seventeenth and eighteenth centuries, and which formed part of the ideological background of the French Revolution.

40. VIRTUE, KNOWLEDGE, AND HAPPINESS: SOCRATES

Socrates (*c.*470–399 BC) was primarily interested in moral problems, as were the contemporaneous Sophists, and like them he was not satisfied with current opinions. He wanted to discover those rules that can be rationally supported; and he was convinced that anyone, by careful reflection, can arrive at an insight into these rules. If we suppose that the dialogues Plato wrote in the period immediately following the death of Socrates reflect Socrates' own ideas, the gist of them would be something like this.

Just as the competent shoemaker is the one who turns out good shoes, so the virtuous man is the one who does what is good. Now every person by each of his actions desires to bring about something he considers to be good. If a person is not virtuous, it can only be because he is in error as to what is actually the good. If a person knew what was really good, he would become virtuous.

How then can this knowledge be acquired? Socrates spoke at times of a warning inner voice, a god or demon (*daimonion*), to whom he listened at critical moments. His most characteristic view, however, was that an investigation of the moral notions is an essential first step on the way to the knowledge of the good.

True happiness (*eudaimonia*) is attained only by living virtuously. The most important thing, therefore, is to tend to the care of the soul and provide it with moral knowledge. Socrates held natural science to be without value for the care of the soul.

It is not without good reason that Greek philosophy is usually divided into a pre-Socratic and a post-Socratic period. Although Socrates did not have a philosophical system to pass on to posterity, he exercised a profound influence upon all subsequent speculation. In one form or another, his concentration upon the mind and his disregard for the outward-looking natural sciences is encountered in most of the post-Socratics, however widely their views may have differed in other respects.

41. VIRTUE AND FATE: THE STOICS

The Stoic school was founded by Zeno of Citium (334–262 BC) at the beginning of the third century BC. (It took its name from the colonnade portico in Athens, adorned with fresco paintings, where Zeno used to lecture, the *Stoa Poikile*.) Chrysippus, who flourished during the latter part of the third century, is considered as the second founder and won fame especially as a logician. In the first centuries AD, Stoicism had many followers within the educated classes of the Roman Empire. Some of the best known of the Roman Stoics were the statesman and teacher of Nero, Seneca, who committed suicide in AD 65; the friend of Emperor Hadrian and former slave, Epictetus (*c.*AD 50–130); and the Emperor Marcus Aurelius (AD 121–80). Each of these wrote Stoic works of edification which have been preserved and are among the noblest of their kind.

The Stoics divided their theory into three major parts: logic, physics, and ethics. We have already considered Stoic logic in the preceding chapter. The essential features of their views on physics were as follows. Only material bodies (*somata*) exist in a genuine sense. Matter remains constant under all changes of state. On the question of the existence of the void, they struck a peculiar middle way between affirmation and denial. The world, i.e. the starry heavens with the earth at their centre, is a sphere beyond which extends an infinite void, but within the world no void exists—the world is everywhere continuously filled by matter. The Stoics adopted and modified the old theory of the four elements. Of special interest is their theory of the *pneuma*, a theory with theological as well as physical aspects. From the point of view of physics, *pneuma* can be described as a subtle, all-pervading substance which is a mixture of fire and air, is the active principle in nature, determines the properties of the bodies it pervades, and by its varying dynamic tension (*tonos*) keeps the world together. (The way the Stoics described their *pneuma* can, as Sambursky has pointed out, easily lead one's thoughts to the ether and field theories of yesterday and today.)

Like Heraclitus the Stoics assumed the periodic recurrence of world holocausts. The entire universe is then destroyed by fire and because of the heat, matter expands until it fills all space. After each holocaust, however, matter is again organized into a new world, which except for minor details is a faithful copy of all previous ones.

The universe is an animated, rational being, and the celestial bodies are also individually animated. The universal spirit, universal reason (*logos*), or God, is both a providence unceasingly concerned for the good of man and the world, and an implacable fate. Providence, or fate, operates in and through the infinite chains of cause and effect. The observable perfection of the world is proof of the existence of the divine Providence.

The Stoics, like Socrates, taught that only virtue is of importance in life. All else is indifferent. The choice between virtue and vice is something that lies in our own power, not that this choice is not causally determined, but in the sense that we ourselves determine the outcome of the choice.

The Stoic "wise" man is he who realizes that the world is constituted as it is described by Stoic physics, and who also realizes that virtue is the only goal truly worth striving for. Armed with this dual insight, he can meet everything that happens to him with confidence, indeed with equanimity. He knows that every blow of fate is the wise decision of providence and that the only important thing, virtue, always depends entirely upon himself. Those who do not possess these insights and this equanimity are "fools".

In many respects the Stoics anticipated ideas and feelings that were later to become part of Christianity. They spoke of God as the "father" of the world and of men as God's "children". As God's children, all men are "brothers". Differences in sex, status, and ethnic group are without significance in comparison with the fact that we are all human beings. Seneca writes: "One says always, 'They are slaves'. No, Men. 'They are slaves'. No, tent comrades. 'They are slaves'. No, friends of a lower status. 'They are slaves'. No, fellow slaves, if you consider that fate has the same power over us all."[1]

Stoicism is a conglomeration of very different ingredients. Perhaps its success can be explained just by its many facets, which made it possible for each person to seize upon what

---

[1] Seneca, *Epist.* 47. 1 ff., in W. Nestle, *Die Nachsokratiker* (Jena, 1923), vol. 2, p. 188.

appealed most to him. The belief in fate could give solace to those who were worried about the results of their actions. The idea that the one important choice—that between virtue and vice—lies in our own power suited the self-confident. The concept of God as the world's good ruler could serve as a source of inspiration for those who ruled over smaller parts of the world, emperors and statesmen. The idea of the equality of all men before God appealed to the little people of the world. In its many-sidedness Stoicism resembled the contemporaneously developing Christianity more than did any other of the ancient schools of philosophy.

42. PLEASURE AND FREEDOM: THE EPICUREANS

The Epicurean school was founded in Athens about 300 BC by Epicurus of Samos (341–270 BC). For several centuries Epicureanism was, on the philosophical level, the most important competitor of Stoicism. A famous disciple of the school was the Roman poet Lucretius Carus (91–51 BC), who in his well-known didactic poem, *On the Nature of things (De rerum natura)*, enthusiastically proclaimed Epicurus' doctrine of salvation.

Epicurus' idea of the universe agrees in its main outlines with the atomistic theory which Leucippus and Democritus first proposed in the fifth century BC. On one point, however, Epicurus changed the original theory in an interesting way. The point was determinism. He, too, maintained that the motion of the atoms is determined on the whole by mechanical laws, but he admitted certain exceptions. At times the atoms make small, unpredictable changes in the direction of their movement. This "freedom" of the atoms is the explanation of the "freedom" we find in our own will.

Epicurus' doctrine of death may already have been held by the original Atomists, but he put an emphasis of his own upon it. When the body dies, the atoms that constitute the soul are dispersed, and therewith consciousness ends. "So death, the most terrifying of all ills, is nothing to us, since so long as we exist, death is not with us; but when death comes, then we do not exist."[2]

---

[2] Epicurus, "Letter to Menoeceus", in W. J. Oates (ed.), *The Stoic and Epicurean Philosophers* (New York: Random House, 1940), p. 31.

The Epicureans were the last representatives of the sort of world view that the old philosophers of nature put forth. On the basis of the atomic theory, they disputed the theological, anthropocentric, and teleological ideas which through Plato had won such a dominant position in ancient thought. They did not, it is true, deny the existence of the gods, but they held that they were beings who maintained themselves in the spaces between the worlds and there enjoyed their blissful existence without concern for what happened in the worlds. The events in our world are not the result of any divine plan but come about from natural causes. Man's weakness and helplessness are evidence enough that the world has not been established for his sake by some providence.

Pleasure is the only good and pain the only real evil. Physical pain is slight or of brief duration—in any case quite possible to bear. The pleasure of the soul is merely freedom from pain. The wise man, who is not misled by superstition and does not vainly strive for indifferent things, easily attains this state of mind, which the Epicureans at times likened to the peace of the sea during a calm. Epicurus said: "Always keep these four medicines close at hand: God is not to be feared; death means the loss of consciousness; the good is easily attained; the evil is readily endured."[3]

Despite their many theoretical divergencies, there is a close relationship between Stoicism and Epicureanism. According to both, the world has no evil intentions towards us: in the opinion of the Stoics, all its intentions are good; in the opinion of the Epicureans, it has no intentions at all. For both, the world cannot dispossess us of what is really worth having. According to the Stoics, this is virtue alone, and it depends on our own choice. For the Epicureans, it is the freedom of the mind from pain, which we can induce in ourselves. Both wanted to give security to man by convincing him that there is nothing to fear, and that it lies in his own power to attain what is worth striving for; both wanted to save him by means of a faith.

---

[3] Nestle, *Die Nachsokratiker*, vol. 1, p. 220.

43. FREEDOM FROM BELIEF: THE SCEPTICS

During the same period that Stoicism and Epicureanism were enjoying their golden age, there appeared on the scene a school of philosophy which proposed a directly opposite way to the salvation of the soul—viz. the freedom from all belief.

Scepticism may in part have simply been an expression of weariness with the bickering of the "dogmatic" schools of philosophy, and perhaps also at times a pose of intellectual superiority (a kind of "one-upmanship"). Undoubtedly, however, there were deeper motives as well. A well-known way of evading an unpleasant fact is simply not to believe it. That thorough critic of scepticism, Bolzano, in his *Theory of Science* (1837), described this motivation in the following way: the danger of yielding to total doubt is "so much greater when this state of doubt is in some respects welcome to us: when we wish that all certainties might disappear from our sight".[4] Seen in this light, scepticism is a form of escapism. This is not to deny that a dose of scepticism is a healthy component of the philosopher's frame of mind.

The sceptics considered Pyrrhon of Elis (365–275 BC) as the founder of their school of thought. According to his pupil Timon (*c.* 325–235 BC), the Pyrrhonist wisdom could be summed up in the form of answers to three questions. What is the nature of things? Pyrrhon's answer was that we do not know. What attitude should we take toward things? Answer: entertain no opinions. What do we gain thereby? Answer: peace of mind.[5]

In the third and second centuries BC, the Academics Arcesilaos (315–241) and Carneades (214–129) levelled a sceptical critique against the "dogmatic" schools of philosophy, especially the Stoics. During the second half of the first century BC, Aenesidemus founded a school of scepticism in Alexandria which was to live on for about 200 years. Sextus Empiricus, a physician who lived in the second century AD, has given us the most detailed extant exposition of ideas of the Sceptics. According to him, the Sceptic accepts those sense impressions and those opinions that, in

[4] B. Bolzano, *Wissenschaftslehre* (Sulzbach, 1837), vol. I, p. 000.
[5] Cf. Nestle, *Die Nachsokratiker*, vol. 2, p. 250.

a manner of speaking, thrust themselves upon him in everyday life. He does it, however, in the same way that the schoolboy accepts his lessons, without any real conviction. On all the questions that the philosophers and the erudite debate, he abstains from having any views; he neither approves of, nor rejects, any view, but practises abstinence from judgement (*epoche*). In order to attain this state of mind, the Sceptic must first set "phenomena and arguments" against each other so that they are dispossessed of their force of conviction.

Against the claim of sense perception to provide us with knowledge of an independent reality, Sextus adduces a long series of arguments. Which sense impression a being receives from an object depends not only on the nature of the object itself, but also on the relations of the object to the apprehender (i.e. the distance and the like), on the constitution of the sense organs, on what condition the apprehender happens to be in (sleeping or waking, sober or intoxicated), and so on.

Against induction the following objections were made. It is complete or incomplete. In incomplete induction we proceed, for example, from the fact that up to now we have observed a great number of mortal humans but never an immortal one, and we conclude that all humans are mortal. We have no assurance, though, that no human who now exists or who ever will exist is not immortal. Complete induction would mean that we first observed every individual human, established his mortality, and then set up the general proposition. Such induction is beyond our powers, however. Thus, induction, if incomplete, is inconclusive and, if complete, impossible.[6]

Sextus also objects to the use of inductively demonstrated propositions in the inference of singular conclusions. Assume that we try to prove in the following way that Socrates is not four-footed:

(i)   No man is four-footed
(ii) Socrates is a man
(iii) Hence, Socrates is not four-footed

---

[6] Sextus Empiricus, *Outlines of Pyrrhonism*, II 15.

where in support of (i) we refer to the fact that Plato, Dion, *et al.* are not four-footed. In order to be certain that (i) is true, according to the Sceptics we must already know (iii). The given proof is therefore worthless.[7]

Against deductive proofs the following objection was raised. Either we start from arbitrary assumptions, in which case the proof is worthless; or else the chain of proofs must be extended backwards *ad infinitum*, which is impossible; or else there is a case of circular reasoning which is also worthless.[8]

Ancient scepticism underwent a renaissance in the seventeenth and eighteenth centuries, when "Pyrrhonism" had numerous followers. Many philosophers were especially attracted by the sceptical arguments against sense perception. Descartes's doubts, as well as Berkeley's and Hume's discussions of the relation of experience to the external world, must be seen against the background of the revival of ancient scepticism. The same is true of Hume's critique of induction. Whereas the ancient Sceptics sought a total freedom from belief, in the seventeenth and eighteenth centuries the sceptic arguments were used to peel off the layers of the doubtful or uncertain in order to arrive at a kernel of absolute certainty in our world of ideas. Since this epistemological problem was studied by Descartes in the seventeenth century it has never ceased to engage the interest of philosophers. On the basis of the certain knowledge which doubt has been thought to leave untouched, philosophers have sought either to substantiate or to refute those other claims to knowledge that preceded doubt. In this manner, the knowledge of other minds, the knowledge of the past, of the future, or of the external world, have been discussed. Substantiation and refutation have followed one upon the other in a confusing sequence. In the results at which a certain philosopher has arrived, it is often difficult to see anything but the outcome of a subjective struggle between doubt and belief. This entire mode of thought, which has been so dominant in the epistemology of modern times but whose fruitfulness is often suspect, has its historical roots in ancient scepticism.

[7] Sextus Empiricus, *Outlines of Pyrrhonism*, II 14.
[8] Ibid. I 16.

The complete doubt which the ancient sceptics thought to be the road to peace of mind has usually been considered an illness. It is a malady which has a specially dangerous attraction for philosophers. In the history of philosophy several attempts are therefore found to adduce reasons which should persuade even the most obdurate Sceptic to change his mind. St. Augustine, Descartes, Bolzano, and G. E. Moore are four celebrated thinkers who have devoted serious attention to this problem of mental hygiene.

44. THE FLIGHT OF THE SOUL FROM MATTER TO GOD:
    THE NEO-PLATONISTS

The neo-Platonic school was founded in Rome in the third century AD by the Egyptian Plotinus (204–69), who was said to have experienced the ecstatic identification with God four times during his life. Ancient philosophy, which began with the Milesians' sober attempt to form a rational picture of the universe, thus culminated in a fantastic mysticism.

"The First" or "the One", the godhead, raised above all multiplicity, is an original cause from which reality evolves through successive "radiations" or "reflections". Some of the most important stages in this process are the timeless Reason which perceives only the First; the Platonic Ideas, which for Plotinus are a kind of spirit, all of which together compose the intelligible world; the First World Soul which encompasses these Ideas; the Second World Soul which is associated with the universe as our souls are associated with our bodies; the individual souls (yours and mine); and finally, matter. The closer to God we get in this sequence, the more light and goodness we encounter; the closer matter is approached, the more darkness and evil is met with. The task of the human soul is to free itself from matter and somehow to ascend to God. The stages in this rise of the soul from matter to God are physical asceticism (fasting, chastity, vigils), contemplation, and, ultimately, ecstasy, the "simplification", when individual consciousness is extinguished and the divine light streams forth.

Neo-Platonism had many adherents and exercised a strong influence until the final victory of Christianity and the beginnings of the Middle Ages. Many of the neo-Platonists were outstanding scholars, such as the Syrians, Porphyry (AD 232–301 or 304) and Iamblichus (c. AD 280–330), the Greek philosopher Proclus (AD 410–85), Simplicius (sixth century AD), the Christian convert Johannes Philoponous (sixth century AD), and the Roman Christian Boethius (c. AD 480–525). They all devoted themselves to the work, highly esteemed during late antiquity, of writing commentaries on the classical works of philosophy and science. Those of their commentaries that were preserved were an important source of knowledge of ancient thought during the Middle Ages, and they still are to us. Boethius' translations into Latin of certain of Aristotle's logical works and his own texts on logic and mathematics were some of the most important contacts with Greek thinking that were available to the scholars of early medieval times. Plotinus' successors, however, showed a disposition for combining all sorts of superstitions with the master's mystical visions. Iamblichus declared, "Doubt not any divine miracle, nor any religious belief."[9]

The turning away of philosophy from empirical reality, which had begun with Socrates, attained its culmination in neo-Platonism, which was the last great non-Christian school of philosophy. The young Christianity borrowed much from neo-Platonism. During the Middle Ages, mystics such as Johannes Scotus Erigena (ninth century) and Meister Eckhardt (c. 1300) were inspired by neo-Platonic ideas.

The academic form of mysticism, which was developed by the German transcendental philosophers at the beginning of the nineteenth century, had many points of contact with the doctrine of Plotinus.

In his biography of Plotinus, Porphyry tells us about the master's lively interest in Indian and Persian wisdom, and says that he even accompanied a military expedition against Persia in order to get first-hand contact with it. In Plotinus the Platonic denial of the world was perhaps strengthened by the even more radical Hindu denial. If so, elements from the philosophy and emotional world of Hinduism have, via Plotinus, influenced Western mysticism from its very inception.

[9] E. Zeller, *Grundriss der Geschichte der griechischen Philosophie* (13th edn., Leipzig, 1928), p. 372.

THE MIDDLE AGES

VII

'Credo ut intelligam'

45. THE AUGUSTINIAN TRADITION

Christianity became the official religion of the Roman Empire in the fourth century AD. Philosophical thought, which for long had been concentrated on the problems of life, was gradually transformed into the hand-maid of Christian theology. The Christian thinkers who were interested in philosophical reasoning speculated as a rule in accordance with the maxim *Credo ut intelligam* (I believe in order that I may understand). They considered their belief to be justified by the Bible, which to them was God's word, by the supernatural events related there, and sometimes by personal religious experiences. They did not think that their belief was in need of justification by profane proofs. By a "profane proof" of a Christian tenet I mean one that proceeds from premises acceptable also to those who do not already share the belief that the Bible is God's word, or that the supernatural events related in the Bible took place in the way described, and who do not claim to have had any specifically religious experience. Nor did the Christian philosophers think that all of the Christian dogma was susceptible of profane proof. Some tenets were held to be mysteries which transcend the bounds of understanding and can be comprehended only through faith. Though no Christian tenet needed to be proved profanely, and not all could be, it was thought desirable to give profane proofs of the most general or fundamental articles of Christian belief, the *preambulae fidei*, whose acceptance was a first precondition for the initiation into the full Christian faith. To this class were generally referred such dogmas as the existence of God, the divine creation of the world, and the immortality of the soul.

One reason why the Christian theologians sought to provide profane proofs for these and similar dogmas was their
wish to refute the opponents of Christianity, or to win them
over. Another, and in the long run the more important,
reason was that they found it more satisfactory to be able
both to believe and to know, or to understand intellectually,
as much as possible of the Christian doctrine. In one part
of their mental life—that part to which they accorded supre-
macy—they accepted the Christian tenets as axioms. In
another part, however, they wished as far as possible to find
proofs and explanations of the dogma. Although it would be
incorrect to say that the Christian philosophers looked only
for profane proofs of the dogma, such proofs were nevertheless always of predominant interest for the Christian philosophical tradition which was inaugurated by Augustine and
attained full development during the thirteenth century with
such thinkers as Bonaventure, Albertus Magnus, Thomas
Aquinas, and John Duns Scotus.

The Christian philosophers made use of the conceptual
schemes and modes of thought that had originally appeared
in classical Greek philosophy. Until the twelfth century,
however, Western Europe had only a very incomplete knowledge of classical philosophy. Of Plato's writings only the
Timaeus was known. Some of Aristotle's minor logical works
were also available. As for the rest of classical philosophy,
most of it was known only indirectly, through the neo-
Platonic commentaries and the often imperfect and tenden-
tious summaries compiled by the early fathers of the Church.
Until the twelfth and thirteenth centuries, when Aristotle's
works became known in more complete Latin translations,
Christian philosophy was more Platonic and neo-Platonic
than Aristotelian. When Aristotle had once become more
fully known, however, he was to exert a vast influence on
philosophy and theology. Many of the most famous
exponents of Scholasticism set themselves the task of achiev-
ing a synthesis of Aristotle's philosophy and the Christian
doctrine. The most celebrated of these Aristotelian
Scholastics is Thomas Aquinas, who lived in the thirteenth
century, and whose system today, after 700 years, is the
official philosophy of the Catholic Church.

46. AUGUSTINE'S PHILOSOPHY

St. Augustine (AD 354–430) is the first great name in the long succession of Christian theologians who tried to support their faith with philosophical argument. Augustine's philosophy can best be characterized as a synthesis of Christian doctrine with Platonic and neo-Platonic thinking. (Certain passages in his works, for instance the treatise *On Free Will*, are even paraphrases of passages from Plato's dialogues.) That Christian theology acquired the legacy of Platonic idealism is due above all to Augustine. As a theologian, he is famed for the historical perspective he developed in *The City of God* and for his theories of predestination, original sin, freedom, and grace. After Jesus (assuming his historical existence), the Evangelists, and St. Paul, St. Augustine is perhaps the one who contributed most to the shaping of the Christian doctrine. In the history of philosophy he has earned a place through such contributions as his criticism of scepticism (where he anticipated Descartes) and his theory of eternal truth.

A. *The refutation of scepticism*

Augustine time and time again attacks the sceptic thesis that we have no certain knowledge. The thesis is of course refuted if we can exhibit some proposition p such that we know for certain that p. Augustine's refutation consists precisely in adducing such counter-instances to the sceptic assertion.

(i) In *Three Books Against the Academics* (Book III), Augustine states that dialectical (i.e. logical) truths are propositions of which we have an absolutely certain knowledge. As examples of dialectical truths he mentions various propositions of the forms, 'not (p and not-p)', 'p or not-p', 'p and q, or not-p and q, or p and not-q, or not-p and not-q'. Mathematical truths also have this highest degree of certainty. That $3 \times 3 = 9$ is a necessary truth of which we are absolutely certain. The objection that while asleep we can make every conceivable mistake and that perhaps our mathematical thinking is all a dream, he dismisses with the retort that $3 \times 3 = 9$ is necessarily true even if all mankind be snoring.

(ii) Of greater historical interest is another refutation of scepticism which Augustine presents in most detail in *On Free Will* (II. 3. vii) and in *The City of God* (XI. 26). In the latter work he states in his studied roundabout manner:

. . . I know without any fantastical imagination that I am myself, that this I know and love. I fear not the Academic arguments on these truths, which say: "What if you err?" If I err, I am. For he that has no being cannot err, and therefore mine error proves my being. Which being so, how can I err in believing in my being? For though I be one that may err, yet doubtless in that I know my being I err not; and consequently, if I know that, I know my being: and loving these two [my being and my knowledge thereof], I adjoin this love as a third of equal esteem with the two.

Augustine does not set up his argument in the form of a regular deduction. If we formalize his reasoning, however, we obtain the following sequence of propositions. He postulates as evident:

A 1. If a person errs in some belief of his, then he exists.

From *A 1* it follows that

(a)   If I err in my belief that I exist, then I exist.

By considering the meaning of error, the following proposition is found to be evident also:

A 2. If I exist, then I do not err in my belief that I exist.

If now we combine propositions (a) and *A 2*, we obtain the conclusion:

(b)   If I err in my belief that I exist, then I do not err in my belief that I exist.

From this it follows, by a rule of logic, which was already known to Plato and Euclid:

(c)   I do not err in my belief that I exist.

This reasoning is an ancestor of Descartes's famous *cogito ergo sum*. Whereas in Descartes's expositions of his philosophy, the *cogito* usually constitutes the one original premiss for all certain knowledge, Augustine considered the proposition, "I exist", as a certain truth on a par with many others, for example the dialectical and mathematical truths.

B. *The intelligible objects and eternal truths of mathematics*

Although Augustine was not much versed in the mathematical sciences, they play an important role in his philosophical speculations. From Plato, and ultimately from the Pythagoreans, he borrowed the idea that numerical relationships are the essence of the sensible world and that all real knowledge thereof must assume a mathematical form. The philosophical aim he set himself was to make the knowledge of God and divine things as clear and distinct as our knowledge of geometrical forms.

Augustine took over from Plato the view that pure mathematics is concerned with a realm of objects that we can grasp only by abstract thought. Like Plato he assumed that the numbers of pure arithmetic are collections of abstract units (in Plato: "monads") which do not occur in the sensible world. Such mathematical truths as: '$6 + 1 = 7$', 'For each number n, the number $2 \times n$ is the nth number in order after n', are eternal, unalterable truths. When characterizing them in this manner Augustine took up a line of thought that had already occurred in Aristotle. A proposition like 'The sun is shining' may be true today but false tomorrow. An eternal truth, on the other hand, is true at every moment of time.[1] In Augustine, as in Aristotle, the notion of necessary truth is intimately bound up with this notion of eternal truth.

Truths of the type that assert something about every number attracted Augustine's special interest. How can we obtain knowledge of such truths? Since the numbers 1, 2, 3 . . . are infinitely many, our knowledge cannot be based on a complete induction. Here, complete induction would look like this:

1 has the property E
2 has the property E
3 has the property E
    etc.
_____

Hence, every number has the property E.

[1] The idea of eternal truth, in the present sense, played an important role in medieval philosophy. According to Robert Grosseteste (12th and 13th cents.), "Something will have existed" is a truth without beginning—it has always been true—as well as a truth without end—it will always be true—and hence it is eternal. In modern logical research, sentences of the present kind have been made the object of a special tense logic. Cf. A. N. Prior, *Time and Modality* (Oxford, 1957).

Obviously, it is humanly impossible to go through each and every one of the infinitely many numbers and establish the infinitely many premisses of such an induction. Although Augustine sometimes shows a certain inclination for the Platonic theory of reminiscence, he rejects if for the reason, *inter alia*, that all men can learn mathematics, but that all men cannot be supposed to have been mathematicians before birth. His own answer to the problem is that we perceive these mathematical propositions by means of an inner light or divine illumination. With the support of Augustine's authority, this theory of illumination came to enjoy widespread popularity during the Middle Ages.

C. *The Eternal Truth*

Besides the many eternal truths, in dialectics (logic), and in mathematics, Augustine speaks of "the Eternal Truth". How is the Eternal Truth related to the many eternal truths? One aspect of Augustine's view can, I think, be explained as an application of the logical axiom schemata of the Platonic theory of Ideas (cf. Ch. II, § 12). Substituting "eternal truth" for "X" in those schemata, we obtain the conclusion that there exists a unique Idea, the Idea of Eternal Truth, such that being an eternal truth is the same as partaking of that Idea. When speaking of the Eternal Truth Augustine seems to contemplate something like this Idea.

Another aspect of Augustine's thought comes to light in his attempt to prove that Truth is eternal. He thinks he can do so by a *reductio ad absurdum* of the opposite supposition. Let us suppose, say, that Truth should cease to exist at some moment of time. At all moments from then on it would be a truth that Truth no more exists, and so Truth would then nevertheless exist. Apparently Augustine here understands the phrases on which the argument turns as follows:

(i) Truth exists at the moment t = df Some proposition is true at t.

(ii) Truth is eternal = df Truth exists at every moment.

The salient point of Augustine's proof is the assumption:

(iii) If Truth does not exist at t, then the proposition 'Truth does not exist' is true at t.[2]

D. *Theological conclusions from the theory of Eternal Truth*

The theory of Eternal Truth was of interest to Augustine above all because of the theological conclusions he drew from it. The proposition, 'The Eternal Truth exists', is an essential premiss for his demonstration of the existence of God as well as for his proof of the immortality of the soul.

The proof of the soul's immortality is short and simple and, it must be admitted, as weak as all other known proofs that have the same aim. The proof breaks down into two main parts. The first part is the step from the premiss:

(P 1) We have knowledge of certain eternal truths,

to the conclusion:

(a) Our souls are the abode of Eternal Truth.

In the second part the following additional premiss is adduced:

(P 2) Something imperishable can have its abode only in something imperishable.

From (a) and (P 2) Augustine infers that

(b) The soul is imperishable.[3]

This proof has a striking resemblance to the magician's trick of extracting a live rabbit from an empty hat. After the first surprise is over, we ask ourselves, "Was the hat really empty?" That is to say, what has Augustine actually read into proposition (a) and postulate (P 2)?

Augustine's demonstration of the existence of God is more complex.[4] Augustine proposes the following definition:

D$_1$. God = df that being than which nothing is higher.

---

[2] H. Scholz, *Mathesis universalis* (Basel/Stuttgart, 1961), pp. 305 ff.

[3] *Solil.* II 2 ff.; *De imm. an.* I ff. Cf. F. Ueberweg, *Grundriss der Geschichte der Philosophie*, vol. 2, *Die patristische und scholastische Philosophie*, 11th edn., B. Geyer (Berlin, 1928; repr. Basel/Stuttgart, 1961), p. 110.

[4] *De libero arbitrio* II 3–15.

From his argument it seems clear, however, that he is in fact using the term 'God' in accordance with a slightly stronger definition.

D$_2$.   God = df that being which is higher than our soul and than which nothing is higher.

In the following reconstruction of the proof, I take the liberty of presupposing this stronger definition. Augustine explicitly adduces the following premiss:

P$_1$.   The Eternal Truth is higher than our soul.

Implicitly he also assumes the transitivity of the relation 'higher than':

P$_2$.   If a is higher than b and b is higher than c, then a is higher than c.

He now distinguishes two possible cases, viz.:
Case 1. Nothing is higher than the Eternal Truth.
Case 2. Something is higher than the Eternal Truth.
If we suppose case 1 to hold, it follows:

(a)   The Eternal Truth is higher than our soul, and nothing is higher than it.

Invoking his definition of God, Augustine—fallaciously—thinks that he can now draw the conclusion:

(b)   The Eternal Truth is God.

If we next suppose case 2 to hold, it must be possible to point to some entity X which fulfils the condition:

(c) X is higher than the Eternal Truth.

From P 1, P 2, and (c) it follows now that

(d) X is higher than our soul.

Augustine thinks—again fallaciously—that (c) and (d) entitle him to infer:

(e) X is God.

Thus, in Augustine's opinion, God exists in each of the two possible cases he has distinguished.

As a moment's reflection will show, the proof is quite inconclusive. Let us call the property of 'being higher than our soul and such that nothing higher exists' the God-property. God is then defined as that being which has the God-property, and the assertion, "God exists" is equivalent to:

(i)   That being that has the God-property exists.

In order to prove this we must prove both of the following propositions:

(ii)   There exists at least one being that has the God-property.

(iii)   There exists at most one being that has the God-property.

Proposition (a) above implies that the Eternal Truth has the God-property, and consequently that (ii) holds. But (iii) has not been proved for case 1. As far as the argument goes, there may exist entities other than the Eternal Truth that also possess the God-property. Turning to case 2 we find that propositions (c) and (d) do not even prove (ii). Notwithstanding (c) and (d), it is conceivable that there exists an infinite sequence of higher and higher beings: our souls, the Eternal Truth, X, X', X'' . . . No member of such a sequence can make claim to the God-property. Those medieval proofs for the existence of God, which we shall study in the next section, take this possibility of an infinite sequence into consideration and explicitly exclude it.

Apparently Augustine thought not only that nothing is higher than God, but also that God is higher than *everything* else. Whatever value one may attribute to the above demonstration, it is clear that it falls short of proving the latter claim.

47. PROOFS BY REGRESSION FOR THE EXISTENCE OF GOD

Augustine's proof of God's existence is based on the assumption of a relation 'higher than'. Augustine apparently thought he could prove that there is a unique being, namely God, who is higher than everything else. In the proofs of God's existence that appeared during the Middle Ages, similar lines of reasoning recur. A binary relation, Rxy, or 'x has R to y', believed to be exemplified in experience, is assumed to fulfil the condition:

I. If Rx_1x_2 and Rx_2x_3 and . . . $Rx_{n-1}x_n$, then x_1 is not identical with x_n ($n = 1, 2 \ldots$).

Concerning such a relation R, a medieval proof by regression (as I shall call it) tried to establish that it orders things or events of the universe in a hierarchical order with God at its peak. Let us say that y is an R-successor of x if $x R y$ holds. The proofs thus imply that, if we start with any thing or event x_1 and go from there to its R-successor x_2, then again to an R-successor x_3 of x_2, and so on, we will always ultimately arrive at God who has no R-successor. If the relation R is supposed to be transitive, i.e. if $x R y$ and $y R z$ generally imply $x R z$, then God will also be an R-successor of everything that at all has any R-successor.

The assumption of such a hierarchical order implies a number of theses which I shall now state and to which, for the sake of future reference, I shall give names. Let us say that a sequence of terms $s = (a_1 \ldots a_n)$ is an R-sequence if S contains at least two terms, and if for every pair of terms a_i and a_{i+1} that belong to s, it is the case that Ra_ia_{i+1}. Let us say that an R-sequence is terminated if there does not exist an x such that Ra_nx.

Let us also say that an R-sequence can be terminated if it is the initial part of a terminated R-sequence. The assumed hierarchical order obviously implies what I shall call the principle of termination:

II. Every non-terminated R-sequence can be terminated.

It also implies what I shall call the special principle of convergence:

III. All terminated R-sequences have the same final term.

Finally, the assumed order implies what I shall call the theological principle:

IV. The common final term of all terminated R-sequences is God.

In the works of Anselm of Canterbury (eleventh century), there occurs a proof by regression for the existence of God, based on the relation:

(R_1xy) x is lower than y (or: y is higher than x).

According to Anselm, this relation is exemplified in experience by a sequence such as stone–horse–man, a horse being something higher than a stone, and a man something higher than a horse. Many of the medieval thinkers believed it possible to demonstrate the existence of God by regression using the relation:

(R_2xy) x is set in motion by y,

God being conceived of in Aristotelian fashion as the Unmoved Mover; or using the relation:

(R_3xy) x is caused by y,

God now conceived of as the first cause; or the relation:

(R_4xy) x receives its existence from y

God now being thought of as that being that does not receive its existence from any other being (or that being whose *essentia* contains its *existentia*); or employing the relation:

(R_5xy) x is maintained in its existence by y.

Thomas Aquinas proves the existence of God on the basis of several of these relations (R_1 to R_4).

When the existence of God is proved on the basis of several relations, as it is by Thomas Aquinas, it is of course necessary, if the arguments are to settle the matter, to assume also what may be called *the general principle of convergence*:

> V. The final term of all terminated R_1-sequences is identical with the final term of all terminated R_2-sequences, R_3-sequences, etc.

Unless V is assumed, we have no guarantee that the distinct regression arguments prove the existence of the same being. It appears, though, that the medieval demonstrators of God's existence were as a rule unaware of the necessity of this principle.

48. THE CONCEPT OF THE INFINITE IN MEDIEVAL
    PHILOSOPHY

Bonaventure gave several proofs that the world has had a beginning in time. In one of these proofs he assumes that new rational spirits are all the time being born to life in the flesh, and that they are all immortal. If the world had not had a beginning in time, today there would, hence, exist an infinite number of rational spirits. To Bonaventure it is obvious, however:

(A 1) There is no set with an infinite number of simultaneously existing members.

By appealing to this proposition, he reaches the desired conclusion that the world must have had a beginning in time.

In another proof of the same thesis, Bonaventure argues thus: if the world had not had a beginning in time, it would have been in existence for an infinite number of years. Let us call this number A. Now, corresponding to any number of years there is a number of months twelve times as large. If the world had never begun, then it would have been in existence for a number of months equal to $12 \times A$. Bonaventure now implicitly assumes:

(A 2) If n is a finite number larger than 1 and A is an infinite number, and if the number $n \times A$ exists, then $n \times A$ is larger than A.

(A 3) One infinite number cannot be larger than another.

With the aid of these presuppositions he once again arrives at the conclusion that the world must have had a beginning in time.[5] The three assumptions on which Bonaventure rests his proofs were, despite occasional doubters, something of a *commune bonum* among the medieval philosophers. If the following assumption is adjoined to (A 2) and (A 3):

(A 4) If n is a finite number greater than 1, and if A is an infinite number, then the number $n \times A$ exists,

it follows, of course, that there exist no infinite numbers.

[5] F. C. Copleston, *A History of Medieval Philosophy* (London, 1972), Ch. 11, cites one of Bonaventure's arguments and gives further references to the original literature.

From (A 2), (A 3), and (A 4) the validity of (A 1) follows. These three assumptions, in fact, entail the even stronger assertion:

(A1') There is no set with an infinite number of elements (whether existing simultaneously or not).

From (A1') we may in turn infer the principle of the impossibility of an infinite regression. I do not know whether Bonaventure himself would have been prepared to accept (A 4) and its implications. The deductions show, however, that the principle of the impossibility of infinite regression was an organic element in the medieval view of the infinite.

Not until the end of the nineteenth century, when Georg Cantor founded the mathematical discipline called "set theory" (*Mengenlehre*), was greater clarity brought to the notions of an infinite set and an infinite number, which in Bonaventure and other medieval philosophers appear in such odd theological contexts. According to Cantor's set theory, (A1'), (A 2), and (A 3) are incorrect, whereas (A 4) is correct. As for (A 1), which is an assertion concerning what exists in time, Cantor's abstract mathematical theory has nothing to say.

49. THE ONTOLOGICAL PROOF FOR THE EXISTENCE OF GOD

The most bewildering of the medieval proofs for the existence of God is the so-called ontological proof, which was first put forward by Anselm of Canterbury. In the spirit of St. Augustine, Anselm defines 'God' as 'that than which nothing greater can be conceived' (*id quo maius cogitari nequit*).

Since we understand this definition of God, God does exist "in the intellect". The question now arises whether he exists only in the intellect or also in reality. If we suppose that he exists only in the intellect, it is still conceivable that he exists also in reality, which is something greater. "If therefore that than which nothing greater can be conceived exists only in the intellect, that very thing than which nothing greater can be conceived is something than which something greater can be conceived, but for sure this cannot be so."[6]

---

[6] Cf. Ueberweg, op. cit., p. 199.

The 'logic' of this argument is exceedingly difficult to grasp. It seems reasonable to interpret Anselm's definition of God as follows:

(i) God = df that which is such that it is inconceivable that something is greater than it.

Anselm apparently confuses the concept of a thing with the thing itself, or the meaning of a phrase with its reference, when, in view of our understanding of the definition, he concludes:

(ii) God—God himself—exists in the intellect.

His next move is to try to refute the assumption:

(iii) God does not exist in reality, hence only in the intellect.

As a basis for the refutation, he assumes:

(iv) It is conceivable that God exists also in reality,

(v) To exist also in reality is greater than to exist only in the intellect.

From these assumptions he seems to conclude:

(vi) It is conceivable that God is greater than God,

and then:

(vii) It is conceivable that something (i.e. God) is greater than that than which it is inconceivable that something is greater.

This he asserts to be impossible, i.e. he thinks that the following is necessarily true:

(viii) It is not conceivable that something is greater than that than which it is inconceivable that something is greater.

Thus, finally, he can infer that supposition (iii) is false, i.e. that God exists also in reality.

As here interpreted, Anselm's argument is a series of (quite obscure) inferences. Of special interest is Anselm's appeal to assumption (viii). If we abbreviate the phrase, 'it is inconceivable that something is greater than a', by the formula '$F(a)$', (viii) is seen to have the form:

(ix) F (that which is such that F (it)).

Does Anselm think that only some special statements of this form, among them (viii), are necessarily true? In that case some argument is clearly needed to show why just these special statements have this special status. Or did he think that all statements of the form (ix) are necessarily true? If such was the case, Anselm just adopted a poor logic. In modern logical parlance, an expression of the form 'that which is such that F (it)' is usually called a (definite) description. The rules governing such expressions have been made the subject of many penetrating studies. Many consistent sets of rules have also been suggested by different logicians; the first and the most famous method of consistently handling descriptions was stated by Bertrand Russell. In no such system does (ix) enter as a theorem.

Since it was first presented, the ontological proof has been the subject of a stubborn debate. The proof was already objected to in Anselm's lifetime by the monk Gaunilo, who thought that, by the same argument, one might prove the existence of an island so beautiful that none more beautiful can be conceived. The proof reappears with various modifications in many medieval thinkers, and also in Descartes, Spinoza, and Leibniz in the seventeenth century. Not until Kant's famous refutation, in *The Critique of Pure Reason* (1781), did the proof become more generally discredited among continental philosophers. (This did not prevent Hegel and the Swedish idealist Boström from reviving it in the nineteenth century.)

50. THE CHRISTIAN TRADITION IN WESTERN PHILOSOPHY

The Christian tradition in Western philosophy, which resulted from the meeting between Christian religion and Greek philosophy and was heralded by Augustine and other fathers of the Church, was at its peak during the Middle Ages. At the same time, the meeting of Greek philosophy with Islam and the Jewish faith gave rise to parallel Islamic and Jewish traditions. The Christian tradition had a new peak in the seventeenth century, in the systems of the continental rationalists, and yet another in the early nineteenth century, in the systems of the German romantics, Fichte, Schelling, and Hegel. The tradition lives on into the present time. A truly enormous number of Christian philosophers have considered it one of their primary tasks to provide some kind of philosophical support for their religious beliefs. It can fairly be said, I think, that the great efforts that so many brilliant intellects have spent on the task of proving, or justifying, or expounding religion have hardly led to results that carry rational conviction.

In modern times the Christian tradition has been confronted by an anti-Christian and at times even generally anti-religious reaction. Because of the social and political power that the Christian churches have long wielded and, in many places, still wield, this reaction has often had to express itself with caution. One of the earliest critics of religion was Spinoza, whose own belief in God had practically nothing in common with traditional Judaism or Christianity. In the eighteenth century many of the philosophers of the Enlightenment were severely critical of Christianity and institutional religion in general. The philosophically most acute of these critics was probably David Hume.

Forms of materialism may be consistent with forms of religion. Epicurus, the Atomist, believed in the existence of immortal material gods, dwelling in the interspaces between the worlds. The materialistic Stoics believed with earnest piety in a divine providence. It was not until the eighteenth century that materialism began to be invoked in support of a radical criticism of religion by the thinkers of the French Enlightenment (Lamettrie, Holbach, Diderot, *et al.*). In the nineteenth century a new wave of materialism arose in Germany as a reaction against the idealism of the romantics, and it brought with it a new critique of religion. Karl Marx, who rejected religion as a form of "alienation", styled himself a "materialist". Materialism, which in itself is such an obscure view, seems to be an unfortunate burden for those wishing to form an unprejudiced judgement on one or other of the religions, or on religion in general.

In the philosophy of our own age, analytical philosophers have criticized religion from a variety of standpoints. Some, like Bertrand Russell, have mainly stressed its supposed incompatibility with science, while others, like the logical empiricists, have tried, by applying semantic criteria, to rule it out as nonsense.

VIII

'Via Moderna'

51. A HISTORICAL SURVEY

In popular expositions, Aristotle is sometimes credited with an undisputed authority over Western philosophers and theologians throughout the Middle Ages. This is a grossly inaccurate view. Not until the end of the twelfth and the beginning of the thirteenth century did he become a dominant force in medieval thought. Until then most of his works were unknown. When they became more fully known, this was an overwhelming experience for the thinkers of the time. In his works they encountered a new intellectual world, filled with subtle conceptual distinctions, conscientiously recorded empirical data, and daring ideas concerning the structure of the universe. In so many respects, Aristotle's philosophy surpassed all other theories known at that time. Perhaps simpler natures read Aristotle as they read their Bible, but the great thinkers of the thirteenth century quite reasonably considered him to be the one who deserved to be listened to above all others. Aristotle's philosophy was in many ways ideally suited as an instrument for a rational formulation of the Christian faith, and since he had no competitors of equal intellectual rank, philosophy assumed a predominantly Aristotelian character. There were facets of this theory, however, that were incompatible with the doctrines of the Church. He taught, for example, that the universe is eternal, whereas the Church held that it had been created by God at a calculated year in history. His views on the immortality of the soul and the law-bound order of nature could be interpreted in such a way as to conflict with the teaching of the Church on final things and miracles. Indeed, at the beginning of the thirteenth century, the study of Aristotle's works on physics met stiff theological resistance. Towards the end of the century, in 1277, the Church felt obliged to condemn a long list of Aristotelian and Averroistic theses.

On the whole the great thirteenth-century philosophical system builders confined themselves to interpreting Aristotle's theories, making them more precise, modifying them whenever it appeared necessary, and utilizing them for the presentation of Christian theology as a rational system. The different systems that were created then were to have their adherents throughout the Middle Ages. However, by the beginning of the fourteenth century the attitudes of the leading thinkers towards the ancient master had already become far more independent. Even though in their discussions they almost always kept an eye on passages from Aristotle, they criticized him freely, and in many fields ideas were developed that went far beyond anything he ever thought of. They also gained a greater, albeit rather peculiar, freedom of the intellect in relation to the doctrine of the Church. These fourteenth-century philosophers at times spoke of themselves as representatives of the *via moderna* (the new way), while regarding the Thomists and other more orthodox Aristotelians of the thirteenth century as plodding along the *via antiqua* (the old way).

It is impossible to set up a clear demarcation between the *via antiqua* and the *via moderna*. All the medieval Christian philosophers were theologians, and they were continually blending philosophy and theology. The wayfarers along the *via moderna* did not constitute a school of unified opinion. What distinguishes the two groups is more a matter of intellectual atmosphere. Among the modernists three important subgroups can be discerned.

(1) *Ockham and the Ockhamists.* The Englishman, William of Ockham (*c.*1280–1349), was the centre of a group of thinkers who held a more sceptical position in theology and ethics than had the system builders of the thirteenth century, who developed the so-called terminist logic to its perfection, and who in semantics defended a nominalist, or conceptualist, theory of general terms in sharp contrast to the Platonic-Aristotelian theory. Along with Ockham, the Frenchmen Jean de Mirecourt and Nicolas d'Autrecourt must also be mentioned here.

The Ockhamists propounded ideas which to a remarkable degree anticipated those of British empiricism in the seventeenth and eighteenth centuries. (There exists here a still unbroken tradition in British philosophy. Even in the time of Locke works by Ockham were used as textbooks in Oxford, and the form of empiricism that Locke inaugurated has never ceased to play a role in British philosophy.) Because of his radical criticism of the Aristotelian conceptual apparatus and his general scepticism, Autrecourt has at times been called the "medieval Hume". Ockham, Mirecourt, and Autrecourt each had many views condemned by the Church, and each duly recanted.

(2) *The Oxford School.* In England, Aristotelianism merges with the previously prevailing Platonic and neo-Platonic tradition. The idea of a mathematical description of nature is far more prominent in the natural philosophy of Plato than it is in that of Aristotle. A long line of English thinkers, headed in the thirteenth century by Robert Grosseteste and Roger Bacon, sought by logico-mathematical methods to solve the problems of natural philosophy, which had then become of current interest through Aristotle's works on physics. In the fourteenth century this work had its centre at Merton College in Oxford. Four of the most prominent names were Walter Burleigh, Richard Swineshead ("the Calculator"), Thomas Bradwardine, and William of Heytesbury. By using terministic logic and essentially geometric methods, they made important progress in mathematical physics and pure mathematics.

(3) *The Paris School.* At the same time, a number of thinkers, such as Jean Buridan, Albert of Saxony, and Nicole Oresme, were working in Paris with similar methods on similar problems.

The intellectual climate in which these modernists worked was characterized by less interest in, and a certain scepticism about, theologico-philosophical systems of the kind developed in the previous century, by enthusiasm for logic, by an inclination to nominalist or conceptualist ideas, by an empiricist tendency, and by an interest in mathematics and a mathematically formulated philosophy of nature. They were in many ways harbingers of the new physics which was to acquire its experimentally verified and theoretically systematized form in the seventeenth century.

52. THEOLOGICO-ETHICAL SCEPTICISM AND THE BEGINNINGS OF EMPIRICISM

The scepticism with which the Ockhamists treated some of the theological and moral tenets of the Church did not, as far as we know, imply that they seriously doubted their truth. Their scepticism went no further than the view that it is impossible to give an adequate profane justification for these tenets, and that, hence, they must be accepted through a faith lacking the character of knowledge, in a profane sense. In the language of medieval philosophy, they withdrew certain questions from the province of "natural theology" and referred them to revelation and faith.

Ockham's own attitude towards the traditional proofs for the existence of God was not so radically negative as has sometimes been thought. Against the proofs by regression, based on the relations 'x is set in motion by y' (R_2xy) and 'x is caused by y' (R_3xy), Ockham objected that both the principle of termination and the theological principle are problematic in this context. These relations can conceivably give rise to unending sequences; and, even if there did exist an unmoved mover, or a first cause, this need not be the God of Christian theology: the unmoved mover could be an angel; the first cause could be a star. Ockham did believe, however, that on the basis of the relations, 'x is simultaneous with, and preserved by, y', and 'x is worse than y', at least incomplete proofs of God's existence can be achieved. It can be proved, he thinks, that there is at least one first preserver, and at least one being unsurpassed in value, but it cannot be proved that there is only one first preserver or only one being unsurpassed in value. In other words, on his view the principle of termination applies to these relations, but it is uncertain whether the principle of convergence also applies to them.[1]

Nicolas d'Autrecourt rejected the proposed proofs for God's existence in an even more radical spirit. In his retraction in 1346 of theories condemned by the Church, he states:

---

[1] *Ordinatio Ockham* and *Quaestiones super libros Physicorum.* Cf. Ockham, *Philosophical writings* (ed. Ph. Boehner, Nelson, 1957), Introduction, p. xliii. Also Ph. Boehner, *Collected Articles on Ockham* (St. Bonaventure, New York, 1958), pp. 150-1.

Likewise, in the forementioned epistle I have said that it cannot be shown with evidence of any thing whatsoever that it surpasses another in nobility.—False.

Likewise, in the forementioned epistle I have said that, taking any indicated thing whatsoever, nobody knows with evidence that it does not excel all others in nobility.—False, heretical, and blasphemous.

Likewise, I have said that, taking any indicated thing whatsoever, nobody knows with evidence that this is not God, if by God we understand the most noble being.—False, heretical, and blasphemous.[2]

The tenets that Nicolas here disavows constitute a shattering and paradoxical critique of all those arguments that purport to prove God's existence from the fact that things vary in worth.

The Christian faith of the Ockhamists influenced their philosophy in an interesting way. They believed in the omnipotence of God, which they defined as follows. Call a state of affairs p contingent if both p and *not-p* are possible. God's omnipotence then implies that (i) God is the cause of every contingent fact p, and (ii) God could have brought *not-p* into existence instead of p if he had so chosen. In other words, logic alone sets bounds to God's might.

Ethical facts are among those that depend upon God's will. That something is good or evil is, on Ockham's view, the very same as God having decreed or forbidden it. Since God can decree or forbid anything whatsoever, *a priori* anything can be good or evil. If God had ordained adultery, which he could have done, then adultery would be something meritorious. Indeed, God could even have commanded mankind to hate him, and if he had done so, then hating God would have been a duty, albeit a duty which, according to Ockham, it would be impossible to fulfil. (To obey God is to love God, and by our very act of doing our duty to hate God, we would love him.) Together with Ockham's definitions of good and evil, the theory of God's omnipotence leads in ethics to the result that only the knowledge of God's will can teach us what is good and what is evil. This result works in the same direction as the rejection of the proofs of God's existence: the scope of reason is narrowed in favour of revelation and faith.

---

[2] J. Lappe, *Nilolaus von Autrecourt*. Beiträge zur Geschichte der Philosophie des Mittelalters, vol. 6:2 (Münster, 1908), p. 33.

If God's omnipotence is, in ethics, a reason for adhering to the Christian faith, then in natural philosophy it becomes a reason for referring to sense experience. When both *p* and *not-p* are possible, God could have willed arbitrarily either of them. It is hence impossible to decide *a priori* which of the opposite states of affairs obtains. In order to know, one must turn to sense experience, to what Ockham called *cognitio intuitiva*.

According to Ockham, any 'singular thing' (substance or quality) can exist apart from any other such thing. There is no contradiction in the supposition that one but not the other of two singular things exists. In conformity with the principle of God's omnipotence, God could thus have willed the one without the other. Reality is not made in one piece, so to speak, but is a mosaic of pieces which have no connection with each other save that which the layer of the mosaic has arbitrarily imposed upon them. This view gives support to the Christian belief in miracles: there is nothing strange about them since God does not have to follow rules. The theory is also a reason why we cannot hope to discover the laws of nature other than simply by observing how God has in fact chosen to arrange the pattern.

The *cognitio intuitiva* I have when I see a star is an absolute thing distinct in point of place and of subject from the absolute thing that the star is. Ockham himself had already hesitated at the question as to what assurance we have that God has chosen to confer existence, not only on the former, but also on the latter thing. Nicolas d'Autrecourt went the entire way along this line of thought and definitely denied that we have any such guarantee. My seeing the star in no way guarantees the reality of the star.

53. THE TERMINIST THEORY OF CONSEQUENCES

The study of formal logic was pursued with great intensity from the twelfth century onwards. The medieval form of logic is the so-called "terminist" logic of which some glimpses will be given in this and the following sections. Peter Abelard (1079–1142) is perhaps the first in whose work some of its basic features can be discerned. In the thirteenth century, two of its foremost representatives were William Shyreswood and Petrus Hispanus, the latter the author of the famous textbook, *Summulae Logicales*. Ockham gave a careful systematic exposition of this logic in his *Summa Totius Logicae*. Among the thinkers who contributed to its development in the fourteenth century, Jean Buridan and Albert of Saxony also hold prominent places. In what follows I shall present some terminist views as they were formulated by Ockham.

According to the terminist conception, logic is part of the science of language. The terminists distinguished two types of constituent in a verbal proposition, the categorematic and the syncategorematic terms. Syncategorematic terms correspond quite closely to what we would today call logical constants, i.e. words such as 'all', 'some', 'is', 'not', 'and', 'either—or', 'if—then'. The categorematic terms similarly correspond to what we now call non-logical constants, words such as 'man', 'stone', and 'animal'. The assumed difference between the two types was that the categorematic terms are names of something, while the syncategorematic terms are not.

By a consequence was meant an expression of the form:

If A and B and . . . , then F,

or

A, B . . . hence F,

where A, B . . . F are propositions. As in the exposition of Stoic logic, it is convenient here to use the symbolic notation:

A, B . . . $\rightarrow F$.

If it is impossible that A, B . . . are all true but F false, such a consequence was said to be "good". As Ockham observed, this convention entails that $A \rightarrow B$ is a good consequence if A is an impossibility (necessarily false) or B a necessity (necessarily true). Two propositions or consequences were considered to be of the same form if they can be transformed into one another by a one-to-one exchange of categorematic terms. The proposition, "All philosophers are wise, and Socrates is a philosopher" has the same form as the proposition "All sharks are greedy, and this is a shark", but not as "All theologians are pious, and Ockham is a logician."

A consequence was said to be formal if every consequence of the same form is good. A good consequence that is not formal was called material. An example of a formal consequence is:

All men are mortal → Some men are mortal.

An example of a material consequence is:

A man is running → A living being is running.

This consequence is material, since a one-to-one exchange of categorematic terms carries it into the following bad consequence:

A stone is heavy → A fly is heavy.

Material consequences were further subdivided in subtle ways which we shall not go into here.

The terminists made their formal consequences the subject of systematic investigation. This fell within the scope of what we would now call propositional logic, and it resulted in a continuation and expansion of the Stoic logic. (The historical connection between Stoic and medieval logic is still rather obscure.) The following are examples from Ockham's logic of what he considered to be formal consequences:

(1) $A \rightarrow A$ or B

(2) A and $B \rightarrow A$

(3) Not $(A$ and $B) \rightarrow$ Not-A or not-B

(4) This man is an animal → Some man is an animal.

(5) All men are animals → This man is an animal.

54. THE PROBLEM OF UNIVERSALS

The problems raised by Plato's theory of Ideas and subsequently discussed by Aristotle and the Stoics, in the context of their semantics, remained at the focus of philosophical interest throughout the Middle Ages. The medieval philosophers whose views in these matters more or less closely agreed with Plato's theory or with Aristotle's modification thereof are usually called (conceptual) realists. We have seen that in Plato the semantic and logical kernel of the theory of

Ideas was embedded in a metaphysics which was partly set forth only in poetic metaphors. To the medieval realists the semantic and logical issues were inseparably connected with questions of Christian theology. According to conceptual realism all men partake of an identical species, 'man'. Original sin could then be construed as follows. In the first man, Adam, the species itself was tainted by sin, and therefore all later men are participants in a sinful species. According to Aristotle's theory of *predicabilia*, one has to distinguish, in a piece of bread and a sip of wine, between their "essences" and their "accidental" attributes. The miracle of the eucharist could now be explained as consisting in the substitution of the essences of Christ's flesh and blood for the essences of bread and wine, while the accidental attributes, here equated with the observable properties, remained unchanged. The zeal with which the doctrine of universals was discussed during the Middle Ages depended, at least in part, on the fact that solutions of the semantic and logical problems were considered to have important consequences for the philosophical understanding of theology.

The prevailing outlook during the Middle Ages was realism. Augustine himself was a Platonist, and his authority helped Platonism to win adherents throughout the epoch. The founders of the great theologico-philosophical systems of the thirteenth century were essentially Aristotelians. As early as the eleventh century, however, thinkers like Roscelin and Abelard were making first approaches towards a theory that radically differed from the Platonic-Aristotelian realism. This mode of thought, usually called nominalistic or conceptualistic, did not attain full development until the fourteenth century, through Ockham and the thinkers associated with him.

55. THE TERMINIST THEORY OF SIGNS

To understand the nominalism of Ockham, it is necessary to have a certain familiarity with the terminist theory of signs, which he employed in stating his theory.

For the terminists, a sign (*signum*) is something that signifies something or has a signification. Three kinds of sign were usually distinguished, namely:

Conventional signs	{ the spoken sign (*terminus prolatus*)
	{ the written sign (*terminus scriptus*)

Natural signs	{ the mental sign (*terminus conceptus,*
	intentio animae).

Different opinions were held concerning the nature of the mental signs. On the view to which Ockham finally adhered, the mental sign is identical with the act of comprehension which takes place in a person who understands the corresponding spoken or written sign.

Just as we can form spoken propositions from spoken signs and written propositions from written signs, so can we form mental propositions from mental signs. There is, so to speak, a mental language running parallel to the spoken and written language. What a mental sign signifies depends upon the intrinsic nature of the sign. A spoken or written sign, on the contrary, signifies something only by virtue of its being associated with a mental sign signifying that thing. Since in principle we can associate any mental sign whatsoever with a given spoken or written sign, the latter can thus, in principle, be given any signification whatsoever. In this sense spoken and written signs are conventional, in distinction to mental signs which are natural.

Signification is a relationship between a sign and the object which it signifies. As conceived by the terminists, this relationship is not a one-to-one correspondence. A given sign may signify several distinct things, and the same thing may also be signified by several signs.

Obviously, anything that a sign may signify will belong to one of the categories indicated in diagram (R). Thus, signs can be classified with respect to which of these categories they (partly or exclusively) take their *significata* from. The terminists indicated the class-membership of a sign by

(R)

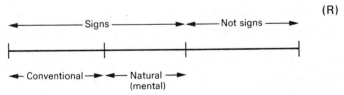

speaking of its kind of "imposition" and of "intention". The details of this classification are complicated and not entirely clear. The following is an account of some distinction as given by Ockham.

A term is of the *second imposition* if it signifies conventional signs exclusively. Examples of terms with second imposition are 'verb', 'conjunction', 'case', 'number', 'mode', and other grammatical terms. A term is of the *first imposition* if it is not of the second. Examples of terms of the first imposition are 'Socrates', 'dog', 'sound'.

Terms of the first imposition can be subdivided in turn into terms of the first and second intention. A term is of the *second intention* if it signifies mental signs exclusively. A term is of the *first intention* if it is not of the second. An example of a term of the second intention is '*intentio animae*'.

Besides the semantic relation of signification the terminists also employed another fundamental semantic relation, namely 'supposition'. A sign's supposition for a thing literally means the sign is taking the place of the thing. Supposition is always relative to a proposition in which the sign occurs. There are many different types of supposition, and the same sign can be of one type in one proposition and of a different type in another proposition. The three most important types of supposition are: the personal, the material, and the simple. A sign has *personal supposition* in a proposition if it supposits there for what it signifies. Thus the word 'man' has personal supposition in the proposition, "Socrates is a man", because it supposits there for men, which it also signifies. In the proposition, "Man is a noun", the same word has *material supposition*, since it now supposits for the spoken or written word 'man'. Finally, in the proposition, "Man is a species", the word has *simple supposition* since it supposits here for the *intentio animae* that signifies men.

56. OCKHAM'S NOMINALISM

Nominalism, as stated in Ockham's works, can be presented in the form of a number of assumptions or postulates, corresponding fairly closely to those postulates through which the Platonic theory was summarized in an earlier chapter.

All of Plato's logical axioms are dropped by nominalism and replaced by the single principle:

I   There exist only individual (singular) things.

In order to give a definite meaning to I, it is of course necessary to add information as to what are admitted as individual things. Ockham seems to have accepted "substances" (e.g. Socrates) and certain "qualities" (e.g. whiteness), but to have rejected the entire Platonic-Aristotelian hierarchy of genera and species together with such entities as quantities, relations, along with much else.

From I follows immediately the semantic corollary:

L. If a sign signifies (supposits for) t, then t is an individual thing.

Consequently, nominalism can no longer accept the condition that Plato laid down for the truth of a singular statement, "a is X". The most characteristic assumption of nominalist semantics is the postulate:

S I   The proposition, "a is X", is true if and only if there exists a thing for which both "a" and "X" supposit in this proposition.

The proposition, "Socrates is a man", for example, is true since the word 'Socrates' supposits here for Socrates, and he is also one of the men for whom the word 'man' supposits.

It is readily seen that S I is closely associated with some of the views on signification cited earlier. The propositions, "Adam is a man", "Cain is a man", "Abel is a man", and so on, are all true. Thus the word 'man', which in all these propositions has a personal supposition, i.e. supposits for what it signifies, will supposit for and signify each and every man: Adam, Cain, Abel, and so on. S I thus overthrows the Platonic postulate according to which the word 'man' is a name of one single thing, the Idea of man. A corollary of S I is the previously mentioned assumption:

S II   There are signs that signify (supposit for) several distinct things.

S I is in Ockham one of several closely related ideas that

together constitute a definition of truth for a comprehensive class of propositions. As the Stoics had done before them, the terminists, including Ockham, formulated truth conditions for conjunction and disjunctions equivalent to our modern truth tables. With regard to the categorical propositions occurring in Aristotelian syllogistic, truth was defined as follows:

S III   The proposition, 'Some X is Y', is true if and only if there is some entity for which both 'X' and 'Y' supposit.

S IV   The proposition, 'All X are Y', is true if and only if 'Y' supposits for every entity for which 'X' supposits.

Ockham also says that 'Some X is Y' ['All X are Y'] is true if 'This X is Y' is true of some [each] particular X one may indicate. Still another explanation is that 'Some X is Y' ['All X are Y'] is true if 'This X is Y, or that X is Y, or . . .' ['This X is Y, and that X is Y, and . . .'], the disjunction [conjunction] taken over all Xs is true. (These explanations were incorporated by the terminists in their complex theory of supposition. 'X' was said to have "definite common personal supposition" in 'Some X is Y', "confused distributive common personal supposition" in 'All X are Y'.)

In view of L, the term "universal thing" or "universal", in the sense of a "non-individual thing", becomes a term without application. It can also be said that this term thus becomes available for purposes other than those for which it was originally introduced by Aristotle. The medieval nominalists thought that the term could aptly be used in accordance with the following definition:

D_1: s is a universal = Df s is a sign signifying several things.

L also gives rise to an analogous situation with regard to the terms "genus", "species", "property", etc. These terms which likewise, because of L, lack application in their original sense, were redefined by the nominalists so as to become applicable to signs. At times these expressions were defined so as to be applicable to conventional as well as to natural signs. In Ockham, however, there is a tendency to limit their applicability to mental signs. Instead of D_1 he often assumes the alternative definition:

D_2: s is a universal = Df s is a mental sign signifying several things.

The terms "universal", "genus", "species", etc. which appear in Aristotle as terms of the first intention, are thus redefined so as to be made terms of the second intention.

57. THE MOTIVATION FOR NOMINALISM AND ITS JUSTIFICATION

In support of his anti-Platonic theory, Ockham adduced a principle of theoretical economy which has subsequently become generally known under the name of "Ockham's razor". The principle can be traced back to Aristotle, and during the Middle Ages it appeared in the writings of several thinkers before Ockham, e.g. in those of his teacher Duns Scotus. Since Ockham seems to have been the first to make an interesting systematic use of the principle, the name may still be kept. Ockham stated the principle in the words: *Non est ponenda pluralitas sine necessitate* (a plurality should not be postulated without necessity), or *Frustra fit per plura, quod potest fieri per pauciora* (it is vain to do with more what can be done with less). With application to conceptual realism the principle is stated as follows: *Sufficiunt singularia, et ita tales res universales omnino frustra ponuntur* (the individual things suffice, and therefore it is totally useless to postulate all those universal entities).[3] Let us call this Ockham's principle of the sufficiency of individual things. Ockham's justification of nominalism is interesting both because of the ideal of theoretical parsimony which he states, and because he points to a criterion by means of which the tenability of nominalism might conceivably be tested.

"Sufficiency" is always sufficiency *for* a certain purpose. What suffices for one purpose may not suffice for another. Ockham's principle of sufficiency therefore needs to be supplemented by an indication of the purpose for which the individual things are considered sufficient. There can be no doubt that it was the following dual purpose:

[3] Cf. Ueberweg, op. cit., p. 576.

(A) Sufficiency for the semantic description of language. Obviously Ockham means that the significance or meaning of language can be described in a satisfactory way without postulating anything but individuals in the range of entities to which language refers.

(B) Sufficiency for the description of the world. It is equally obvious that, in addition to (A), Ockham considers it possible to give a satisfactory description of the world without postulating entities other than individuals. We need not assume, for example, that along with individuals there exist non-individual species and genera. Since semantics is a part of science as a whole, (A) is, of course, a special case of (B).

The concept pair individual–universal can be traced back to Aristotle's development of the Platonic theory of Ideas. Aristotle's explanations of the two concepts is hardly satisfactory. An acceptable explanation of the concepts should enable us to decide, at least in principle, when something is to be classified as an individual and when as a universal. So long as such an explanation is not at hand, the entire discussion for and against nominalism suffers badly from imprecision. Let us now ignore this imprecision, however, and argue as if the necessary explanation had already been supplied. Under this fictitious presupposition, let us consider whether Ockham's assumptions (A) and (B) are justified.

With regard to (A), it may suffice here to collect some of the difficulties that have been brought to light by the history of philosophy. When presenting Stoic logic in Chapter V, we saw that the so-called Electra paradox, which the Stoics debated, seemed to indicate that in semantics a distinction should be made between the objective reference of language, on the one hand, and its linguistic meaning on the other. We also found that the Stoics actually made such a distinction, though possibly without any conscious association with the paradox. While they thought that what language refers to are individual bodies, on the level of linguistic meaning they recognized such abstract entities as properties.

It is relatively easy to see how Plato's conceptual realism can be made semantically impartial, so to speak, with regard to class and relation words. It is more difficult to handle relation words within Ockham's theory, which was primarily stated with regard to class words. Concerning the statement, 'Socrates is similar to Plato', Ockham maintains that it is equivalent to some conjunction, such as 'Socrates is white, and Plato is white'. Whatever the plausibility of this suggestion might be, it is obviously inapplicable to relation statements such as, 'Socrates taught Plato.' According to other statements of Ockham's, a relation name signifies not single things, but pairs of single things. If this theory is elaborated in consistency with Ockham's general theory of signification, it appears that pairs of things must be treated as singular things. Now, if a is greater than b, b is not greater than a. Hence, if a term like 'superiority in size' signifies the pair a-and-b, it does not signify the pair b-and-a. This presupposes that it is possible to distinguish between the pair a-and-b and the pair b-and-a. How this distinction can be upheld from a radically nominalistic point of view seems a bit puzzling. Of course, all so-called non-symmetrical relationships offer the same problem.

Since (A) is a special case of (B), the remarks just made are relevant in forming an opinion about (B) too. Let us see what may be said about (B), however, if we disregard the specifically semantic aspect of the question. If (B) is correct, it would never be necessary to make statements in science such as:

(i) . . . the (universal) entity, A . . .

or:

(ii) There exists some (universal) entity, X such that . . . X . . .

But in science, the highly developed science of our time as well as the rudimentary science of Ockham's days, such formulations are very often used in ways which appear legitimate. From Ockham's standpoint, it apparently becomes incumbent to offer substitutes for, or reinterpretations of, these nominalistically reprehensible statements (i) and (ii). Ockham's way out seems to be the suggestion that the talk of properties in (i) and (ii) should be replaced by talk of signs. More precisely, his theory suggests that (i) and (ii) should be construed as referring to mental signs, *intentiones animae*, rather than to spoken or written signs. In so doing, Ockham assumes signs to be individual things.

Ideas reminiscent of nominalism as developed by Ockham in the fourteenth century have been championed later by such British philosophers as Hobbes and Locke in the seventeenth century, Berkeley and Hume in the eighteenth century, Bentham and John Stuart Mill in the nineteenth century, and by the English biologist Woodger of the present century. Among modern logicians, the Americans Quine and Goodman have endeavoured to construct semantics, formal logic, and mathematics on a nominalistic basis.[4]

58. OCKHAM'S PSYCHOLOGY OF UNIVERSAL CONCEPTS

The Platonic theory, which the nominalists reacted against, also has a psychological aspect. It asserts that in human mental life there exist abstract experiential contents as well as concrete. Those who take an anti-Platonic stand on the problem of universals cannot avoid adopting a position on this Platonic psychology as well. For the eighteenth-century nominalists, Berkeley and Hume, the proof of the non-existence of abstract ideas, i.e. the repudiation of the Platonic psychology, was even the major interest. The anti-Platonists of the Middle Ages were less preoccupied with psychology, but they nevertheless held views on the matter.

Ockham's thinking on this issue underwent an interesting development. Originally, he assumed that in understanding, say, the word 'man' we conceive of something that (i) is

---

[4] Ockham's nominalism was concerned with what medieval logicians called categorematic terms. Remember that in the statements "Socrates is mortal", "All men are mortal", the terms "Socrates", "mortal", and "men" are categorematic, whereas the words "is" ("are") and "all" are syncategorematic. Only the categorematic terms were supposed to have an independent signification. The syncategorematic terms, although lacking signification, somehow contribute to the meaning of the sentences in which they occur. The controversy between the medieval realists and nominalists concerned the question whether universal categorematic terms, such as "man" and "mortal", are unambiguous names of universal entities (realism) or ambiguous names of individual things (nominalism). It is of interest here to note that Quine in our time has proposed an even more radical form of nominalism than the medieval one. According to a suggestion of Quine's, all names (in a suitably standardized language) are unambiguous names of individuals. The universal terms that the medieval logicians treated as categorematic are, by this proposal of Quine's, downgraded to the syncategorematic class.

distinct from our act of conceiving or thinking, (ii) exists merely as conceived by us ("its being is its being conceived"), and (iii) somehow indifferently represents, or bears similarity to, each and every individual man. Ockham calls this mere thought-content a *fictum*, something merely imagined, and he identifies it with the universal mental sign. The theory can be illustrated by diagram (S), where the double arrow stands for the relation between a mental act and its content and the

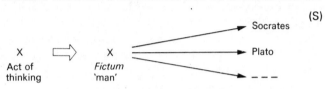

(S)

simple arrows stand for signification. However, Ockham was to find that this view of the matter militates against his principle of intellectual economy. He then dropped the *fictum* and assumed that (a) the act of thinking that constitutes our understanding of the word 'man' by itself, without the mediation of a thought-content, signifies each and every man, and (b) this act is itself the universal mental sign.

59. NATURAL PHILOSOPHY IN THE FOURTEENTH CENTURY

It is impossible to give an account that is both brief and fair of natural philosophy in the fourteenth century. An attempt, such as the following, to indicate its major trends will of necessity be highly subjective. The number of active thinkers was very great. Their mutual dependence was strong but is difficult to ascertain today. Each new idea was quickly seized upon and varied in many different ways. I believe, however, that the following ideas are among the most interesting of those set forth in the fourteenth century in Oxford, Paris, and other European centres of learning.

A. *New mathematical ideas*

When an object is heated, it has different degrees of temperature at different instants. A moving body attains different velocities at different moments of time. The density of matter in a certain body may vary from one point to another, just as it may also vary in time. In all these examples there occurs, in Aristotelian terminology, a "form" of heat, velocity, or density, the intensity of which varies in one way or another. In these and in similar cases, the natural philosophers of the fourteenth century spoke of the *latitudo formarum*, literally the width (breadth) of forms (qualities).

About the middle of the century, Nicole Oresme devised a graphical method of illustrating the *latitudo formarum* which essentially coincides with our modern method of indicating functions by graphs. According to Oresme, our figure (T) can symbolize the variation of the velocity of a body which, in modern terminology, has constant acceleration. The vertical line segment upon t_1 symbolizes the velocity v_1 at time t_1, and so on.

(T)

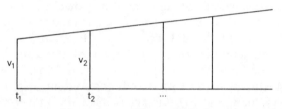

A form was said to be *uniform* if it has everywhere the same intensity, *difform* if the intensity varies. A difform quality can in turn be either uniformly or difformly difform. Figure (T) above illustrates a uniformly difform velocity, whereas figure (U) may illustrate a difformly difform one.

(U)

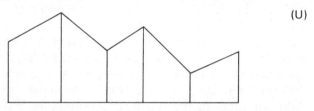

The concept of latitudo is the nearest analogue in the fourteenth century of the modern mathematical concept of a function. The distinctions just referred to can also be readily associated with different types of functions recognized in modern mathematics: a uniform quality corresponds to a constant function, a difform quality to a non-constant function: uniform difformity corresponds to functions having constant derivatives; and so on. Some of the fourteenth-century thinkers went as far as to distinguish also between uniformly and difformly difform difformity, a distinction corresponding to the modern one between constant and non-constant second derivatives. (Of course, there is no strict identity between the medieval and the modern notions.)

With the use of these concepts, a number of interesting kinematic theorems were proved at Oxford, among others the theorem that the distance covered in a given time by a body moving with uniformly difform velocity is equal to the distance covered by a body in the same time when its velocity equals that attained by the former at the midpoint of the time. Oresme also used his graphical method to sum convergent infinite series, and thus he showed, for example, that a finite quantity of matter can fill an infinite space, and that it can be annihilated in a finite time merely through continuous attenuation.

The nature of continuity was also the subject of spirited discussion. Problems of the following kind were eagerly debated. Let the continuum AB be bisected at the point M, as indicated in figure (V), and let the direction left–right represent the relationship less–more (lighter–heavier, earlier–later, etc.). The point M itself may then be referred to either

(V)

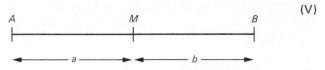

the "lower" left-hand segment a or the "higher" right-hand segment b. In the former case, M is said to be the *maximum quod sic* for a and the *maximum quod non* for b: in the latter case, M is called the *minimum quod non* for a and the *minimum quod sic* for b. Now assume that a represents those weights that Socrates is capable of lifting, and b those that he is not capable of lifting. What then is the character of the boundary point M? Or again, assume that a represents the time during which an object exists and b the time when it exists no more; how should M be classified here? These problems are discussed with considerable logical and mathematical acumen, but on the basis of premises which to us seem rather curious. It was clearly recognized that the existence of a *maximum quod sic* for *a* precluded the existence of a *minimum quod sic* for *b*.

B. *Matter and space*

According to Aristotle, the universe is a finite sphere everywhere filled with matter. Two examples of views that were in conflict with this Aristotelian theory may be mentioned here. Autrecourt defended the atomistic theory, and Oresme assumed that the material world is embedded in an infinite vacuum.

C. *The nature of motion*

For Aristotle, motion was an actualization of something potential. This way of regarding motion was scarcely a fruitful basis for physical theory. Among the many attempts in the fourteenth century to explain the nature of motion, Ockham's was perhaps the most similar to that of modern mathematical physics. He suggested, again using his razor, that motion could be completely characterized by the concepts of time and position. To move is "to have first one position and then another without any intervening state of rest . . . and to continue in this way steadily . . . Consequently the entire nature of motion can be saved by a body's successively being in different positions and not coming to rest in any of them."[5]

D. *The laws of motion*

In his mechanics, Aristotle made use of such notions as force and resistance, without giving definitions to make measurement of them possible. Nor did the fourteenth-century physicists succeed, or even try, to bring these and similar ideas down from the plane of intuition to the level of the experimentally verifiable. Nevertheless, their discussions of mechanics are not without interest.

Force, for Aristotle as well as for the fourteenth-century physicists, determines a body's velocity, and not, as according to Newton, its acceleration. When a body ceases to be

[5] Cf. P. Duhem, *Le Système du monde*, histoire des doctrines cosmologiques de Platon à Copernic, vol. 7 (Paris, 1956), pp. 338–51.

affected by some force, it comes automatically to a state of rest. Suppose that a body of given mass, or "size", is affected by a constantly impelling force f and a resistance r. The fourteenth-century physicists were hardly justified in assuming that Aristotle took its velocity v to be given by the equation:

(i) $$v = k\frac{f}{r} \ (k \text{ a constant}),$$

provided that f is not less than r. This equation is peculiar since, when f equals r, v equals k, whereas, according to the principles of Aristotelian physics, it should, it seems, equal 0. Attempts were therefore made to find a more satisfactory equation. The Englishman Bradwardine suggested, though in different terminology:

(ii) $$v = k \log\left(\frac{f}{r}\right).$$

The Italian Marliani proposed the more trivial:

(iii) $$v = \frac{(f-r)}{r}.$$

Projectile motion was a difficult problem from Aristotle's point of view. When a stone is thrown, it continues to move through the air after leaving the hand. It must thus still be influenced by some force, but which? Aristotle thought that, in some manner, the air carries the stone forward. The neo-Platonist Philoponus had already proposed a notion which under the name of 'impetus' appeared in many variants during the fourteenth century. The theory of impetus, in its general form, asserted that the hand passes on to the stone a motive force, an impetus, which keeps the stone in motion after it has left the hand. Buridan supposed that impetus in itself is unchanging, but that under terrestrial circumstances it is worn away by resistance. Under celestial circumstances, where there is no resistance, a given impetus can maintain motion indefinitely, and Buridan thought that this explains the everlasting motion of the celestial bodies. His version of the theory is evidently closely akin to the Galilean–Newtonian law of inertia.

Concerning free fall, Oresme reached, on theoretical grounds, the same conclusion Galileo was to prove experimentally in the seventeenth century, viz. that the velocity at each moment is directly proportional to the elapsed time of fall.

E.   *Approaches to a new astronomy*

Several objections were made by the Paris school to the Aristotelian theory that the earth is at the geometric centre of the universe. Both Buridan and Oresme thought that it must be the earth's centre of gravity and not its geometric centre that coincides with the universe's geometric centre. For various reasons, the earth's centre of gravity is continually changing, and therefore the earth must also be continually moving in relation to the centre of the universe. In his work, *Du ciel et du monde*, Oresme developed with great clarity the idea that it is more probable that the earth rotates daily about its axis than that the universe daily revolves about the earth.

The fourteenth century was thus burgeoning with interesting ideas on mathematics, physics, and astronomy. Although the discussions of the learned Scholastics were not brought into contact with experimentation and measurement, they did constitute an important stage in the development of mechanics from Aristotle to Galileo and Newton.

Index